An Introduction to Trade and Globalisation

AN INTRODUCTION TO TRADE AND GLOBALISATION

EAMONN BUTLER

Institute of
Economic Affairs

First published in Great Britain in 2021 by
The Institute of Economic Affairs
2 Lord North Street
Westminster
London SW1P 3LB
in association with London Publishing Partnership Ltd
www.londonpublishingpartnership.co.uk

The mission of the Institute of Economic Affairs is to improve understanding
of the fundamental institutions of a free society by analysing and expounding
the role of markets in solving economic and social problems.

A CIP catalogue record for this book is available from the British Library.

ISBN 978-0-255-36803-2

Many IEA publications are translated into languages other
than English or are reprinted. Permission to translate or to reprint
should be sought from the Director General at the address above.

Typeset in Kepler by T&T Productions Ltd
www.tandtproductions.com

Printed and bound by CPI Group (UK) Ltd, Croydon, CR0 4YY

CONTENTS

THE AUTHOR

Eamonn Butler is Director of the Adam Smith Institute, one of the world's leading policy think tanks. He holds degrees in economics and psychology, a PhD in philosophy, and an honorary DLitt. In the 1970s he worked in Washington for the US House of Representatives, and taught philosophy at Hillsdale College, Michigan, before returning to the UK to help found the Adam Smith Institute. He has won the Freedom Medal awarded by Freedoms Foundation at Valley Forge and the UK National Free Enterprise Award; his film *Secrets of the Magna Carta* won an award at the Anthem Film Festival, and his book *Foundations of a Free Society* won the Fisher Prize.

Eamonn's other books include introductions on the pioneering economists Adam Smith, Milton Friedman, F. A. Hayek and Ludwig von Mises. He has also published primers on classical liberalism, public choice, capitalism, democracy, the Austrian School of Economics and great liberal thinkers, as well as *The Condensed Wealth of Nations* and *The Best Book on the Market*. He is co-author of *Forty Centuries of Wage and Price Controls*, and of a series of books on IQ. He is a frequent contributor to print, broadcast and online media.

INTRODUCTION

Who this book is for

This book is a straightforward introduction to the principles, economics and politics of international trade. Written in plain language, it should appeal to intelligent readers who are interested in the principles underpinning the international economy and the public debate about how trade is structured and managed. School and college students, as well as those in business and public policy, should all find it useful.

Why trade and globalisation are important

International trade has grown hugely over the last half century. It has become an extremely important part of modern life, spreading prosperity and promoting interdependence and cultural exchange between nations in a process we call globalisation. It shapes how we live, both as consumers and producers, and provides us with new products and opportunities. And trade is no longer limited to commodities such as cotton, cereals, timber or iron ore: it has expanded into services such as finance, insurance, education, telecommunications, healthcare, tourism, transport, consultancy and information technology.

The interdependence that is essential to globalisation makes possible everyday products such as phones, trainers, cars or office chairs, which now contain components manufactured and assembled in several different countries by many different companies. Manufacturing and retail are in turn made possible by finance, insurance and transportation, services supplied by banks and companies that are also part of a global network. As consumers, we hardly notice this dependence on other countries – at least, until trade is disrupted, and we can no longer access the products we rely on.

With that economic interdependence has come social and cultural exchange. Through trade and globalisation, we can enjoy the whole world's food, movies, theatre, music, art, ideas and learning. And this globalisation has brought a better understanding of other countries' history and traditions, and a greater respect for other ways of life.

Trade and international politics are increasingly entwined. Nearly all economists agree that the best trading regime is open, competitive free trade – a policy of allowing goods and services to be traded between countries with as few restrictions as possible. Politicians, however, often take a different view. This book accepts the economic case for free trade, while seeking to understand the concerns of its critics, such as jobs moving abroad, potential security threats and substandard imports. The book seeks to understand the motives of the critics, while showing the wider damage done by their political responses such as import taxes, embargoes and trade wars.

In summary, trade is an increasingly important subject. Getting trade right is not just a matter of good economics: it is also about how we can peacefully collaborate with millions of other people around the globe.

Structure of the book

The book starts with an outline of the basic principles of trade. Chapter 1 explains that trading is a universal human activity which promotes specialisation and the efficient use of resources. It can, however, create winners and losers and thus lead to criticism and to policies designed to thwart trade. The role of international companies and the morality of free trade are outlined before considering the future of trade.

The next two chapters look at the origins and expansion of trade. Chapter 2 shows how trade goes back to the Stone Age and grew through to modern times. But as chapter 3 explains, the growth of international trade has not always been smooth. In Europe, for instance, medieval restrictions lasted into the nineteenth century before giving way to a century of relatively free trade, until twentieth-century wars led to restrictions being reimposed. Nor have countries' international dealings always been positive. The era of colonialism and imperialism, for example, saw the exploitation of peoples and resources, and the trading of human slaves – things that no advocate of free trade would condone today.

Chapter 4 outlines the theory of trade and countries' specialisation in their 'comparative advantage' capabilities. It explains how trade helps compensate for differences in climate and resources and explores why countries trade with each other. Chapter 5 looks at the benefits from trade, not merely the choice and value it gives to consumers, but the systematic improvement in resource use that it promotes. The chapter also looks at the non-economic benefits of an open trading environment.

The next two chapters raise some of the concerns that people have about trade. Chapter 6 shows that economic change creates winners and losers. Outsourcing production to cheaper countries can threaten jobs, and it may take time for an economy to adjust to new realities. Chapter 7 addresses the concerns that, in a globalised economy, poorer countries are pressurised by richer ones. It explores the concerns that poorer countries may always lag behind, that poorer workers are exploited and the ability of the 'fair trade' movement to redress this, and the issue of rich countries exporting tasks to poorer ones with lower environmental standards.

The next three chapters look at protectionism. Chapter 8 outlines the politics behind protectionist measures, and the measures themselves, before pointing out the costs and unintended results of such policies. Chapter 9 looks in more detail at the arguments for trade barriers: infant industries, dumping, product and labour standards, security concerns – while concluding that most of these are misconceived. Chapter 10 looks at the balance of payments and why deficits are a bad excuse for protectionism.

The following three chapters look at trade today. Chapter 11 points out the current world commitment to lowering trade restrictions, and the broader scope of trade today. It looks at different ways of making trade freer. Chapter 12 looks at global value chains and the role and power of transnational corporations. Chapter 13 explores the moral arguments around trade.

Chapter 14 considers the future of trade. It argues that trade brings general benefits but can also bring losses to specific industries and workers; and that these problems lead to political pressure to restrain trade. It suggests that government policy should not be to restrain trade, but to enable people to adapt to economic change.

1 THE NATURE OF TRADE

Trade is (and was) everywhere

The growth and extent of world trade today is staggering. In 1979 trade accounted for just over a third (35.6 per cent) of world output. By 1999 it was just under half (46.5 per cent), and by 2019 it was well over half (58.2 per cent). In 1999, the total value of goods exported was under $6 trillion and the total value of services exported was little more than $1 trillion. Twenty years later, these totals were nearly $19 trillion and over $6 trillion, respectively (World Bank 2019). Despite inevitable temporary setbacks (financial crises, civil wars, international wars, trade wars, even pandemics), trade seems set to continue its long-term expansion. And with expanding trade has come globalisation – the interaction and integration between the world's peoples, companies and economies, bringing rising prosperity and the spread of ideas, cultures and progress.

Trade has always existed. There is evidence of it going back to the Stone Age, and of astonishing ancient trade networks that crossed and connected entire continents. For millennia it flourished as barter, the direct exchange of goods, before the use of money became more common and the Mediterranean economies took off.

Specialisation and efficiency

Yet the growth of trade was not always smooth. In the medieval era and right up to the eighteenth century, countries thought it better to amass gold and silver than use it to buy foreign goods. It took the great Scottish economist Adam Smith (1776) to demonstrate that both sides gained from trade. His ideas prompted the removal of trade barriers and the great nineteenth-century era of relatively free trade and rising affluence.

Building on another of Smith's insights, that specialisation massively improves our productivity, David Ricardo (1817) showed that countries should focus on what they do better – their comparative advantage – and trade their surplus with others. Through specialisation and trade, in fact, countries can overcome their geography and climate: a cold country can exchange its manufactures for winter fruit, a barren island can trade its minerals for grain.

Concerns over winners and losers

There is no progress without change, but change creates both winners and losers. While Smith is right that both sides must benefit from any single exchange – they would not agree to it otherwise – specialisation and improvements in productivity demand changes that can prove challenging. People in wealthier countries, for example, complain that cheaper foreign workers are taking their jobs, while poorer countries worry that traditional crafts are being driven out by mass produced imports. But it makes no sense for a country to manufacture goods at home when it can buy the same goods or better more cheaply from others. By specialising, every country improves its productivity and its long-term prospects. The competition brought by trade is the spur for this progress.

Critics also fret that richer countries may dominate trade and leave others behind, that poorer workers are exploited in 'sweatshop' conditions or that cultures are being swamped because of trade. In reality, trade has delivered, particularly to the world's poorest, history's biggest and fastest rise in prosperity. The outsourcing of manufacturing tasks to cheaper countries has given the people of those countries new employment opportunities that are less arduous and dangerous than traditional occupations such as farming or mining, and it has allowed them to build richer lives. Trade has also made the world culturally richer than ever before, and it has spread ideas and innovation far and wide.

Protectionism

Nevertheless, although producers are far less numerous than consumers, the pressure from producers who are threatened by cheaper or better goods from abroad leads many countries to put up barriers against foreign competitors. Some countries may want to make themselves self-sufficient, resisting cheaper imports until their own industries grow large enough to compete. They may accuse others of 'dumping' cheap goods on them, undermining their own producers. They may object to imports from countries that do not share their own high employment or environmental standards. They may be worried that they are spending more on buying goods from other countries than those others spend on buying from them.

Whatever the reason, countries often impose taxes ('tariffs') or limits ('quotas') or less obvious barriers in order to stem the flow of foreign imports. But there are costs to this. A large bureaucracy is needed to police the flow. And countries that impose trade barriers make their own populations worse off, because it makes imported goods, which their consumers want and their producers need, more expensive or even unobtainable. Local alternatives might not exist or might be poorer quality. Hence, economists today generally agree that, whatever the temporary benefits for a few producers, such 'protectionism' is a mistake.

Efforts to reduce trade barriers

Protectionism accelerated as a result of World War I, when trade barriers became a weapon to ruin the economies of enemy countries. It dragged on through the interwar years, contributing to the tensions that precipitated World War II. Soon after that, though, the Western powers in particular realised the damage that trade barriers caused and the benefits that reducing them could bring. They set up an international forum – the General Agreement on Tariffs and Trade (GATT) – to discuss ways to limit protectionism and promote easier, freer trade.

> Few propositions command as much consensus among
> professional economists as that open world trade in-
> creases economic growth and raises living standards.
> — Gregory Mankiw (2006)

As more and more countries joined the talks, and new trade
issues rose up the agenda (e.g. trade in services, including
digital and telecoms, the question of whether each country's professional standards should be accepted internationally, the protection of intellectual property), the GATT
talks morphed into a formal international body, the World
Trade Organization (WTO). Over the years, GATT and the
WTO have greatly reduced the average tariffs on imports.
Certainly, high tariffs remain, such as the EU's tariffs on
agricultural products; and trade wars still happen, as between China and the US during the Trump presidency. But
where protectionism exists today it is mostly conducted
through less obvious means – and as such is all the trickier
to deal with.

Transnational corporations

A feature of expanding trade has been the growth of transnational corporations (TNCs). That is because supply or
'value' chains have become truly global.

The iPhone, for example, is assembled in Taiwan. But
the batteries are supplied by a South Korean firm which
manufactures in 80 countries, including India and Brazil.
The sound chips come from another 8 countries, including
the UK, China and Singapore. The screens are made by a US

company, with 107 locations in 24 countries. The gadgets that detect movement come from Germany, China, Japan and several other countries. The gyroscopes are Swiss. The cameras come from US and Japanese corporations with plants in Brazil, China, Indonesia, India and many other countries. The compasses are made by a Japanese firm with factories in France, the US, the UK and elsewhere. A further 27 components come from an equally bewildering range of countries (Krueger 2020: ch. 19).

Managing global networks such as these requires businesses with global reach, working with partners and contractors of all sizes in many different countries. Some critics worry about the economic power that such corporations wield, and whether they can be effectively controlled by any government. Yet transnational operations have always existed, and many are merely loose international collaborations, and less powerful than is commonly supposed.

Trade as a moral good

Many people, then, are suspicious of trade and its effects on poorer countries and peoples, and some even condemn it as a moral evil. But trade has contributed massively to human prosperity, particularly for the very poorest. Since trade began to expand sizeably in the 1990s (when reforms in India, Eastern Europe, Latin America, Africa, East and South East Asia brought those regions more deeply into world trading networks), roughly a billion people have been taken out of $2-a-day poverty.

Trade delivers non-economic benefits too. There is good evidence that it promotes international trust, cooperation and understanding. It is associated with political freedom, the rule of law, honesty, free speech and other liberal values. It even defuses nationalism and ethnic conflict, and promotes peace, fairness and equality. After all, people who want to reap the benefits of trade must learn to cooperate.

And cooperate we do, on a scale unimaginable until now. Even the food we eat adopts the styles and ingredients of the many countries in this globalised world. Film, art and other elements of culture have become international. We have more appreciation of the diversity of other countries and their lifestyles. Companies have become transnational and talented expatriate workers travel and settle in places all over the globe.

The future of trade

As trade has expanded, it has raised new issues. One is a rising focus on security: the US and UK, for example, ban mobile providers from importing Huawei 5G equipment for fear it could be used to spy on their networks. Another is the spread of counterfeit and pirated goods, including clothes and shoes, electronics, perfumes, toys and medicines, which the Organisation for Economic Cooperation and Development estimates at over 3 per cent of world trade (OECD 2019). A growing part of trade is now services, such as banking, accountancy, legal services, healthcare and education, digital services and telecommunications, raising issues of their own as well as the general question of whether the qualifications of the relevant professionals (such as lawyers and accountants) should be accepted internationally. Another concern is the environment, with countries resisting imports with high carbon footprints or banning the importation of certain fertilisers and pesticides. And more generally, the growth of 'emerging' economies (such as Brazil, China, India, Indonesia, Mexico, Morocco, the Philippines, South Africa and Turkey) is tilting the traditional economic balances between regions across the globe.

Sadly, most policy on trade is driven not by economic logic but by domestic and international politics. That is why trade needs an international framework, and a global rule of law, to work well. This is no easy task, given the many pressures on countries to protect their own industries and raise barriers against others. But we have no way of knowing where trade will take us in the future: our best policy is not to resist change, but to help those affected to adapt to it.

PART ONE

THE RISE OF TRADE

2 THE ORIGINS OF TRADE

Stone Age trade

Trade is as widespread as humanity, and probably as old. We certainly know that Stone Age blades and tools made of obsidian, a hard volcanic glass, were transported around what are now the New Guinea islands as long as 20,000 years ago (Summerhayes 2009) and around the Mediterranean as long as 17,000 years ago (Atakuman et al. 2020). Some 8,000 years ago, Turkish wheat was being exported to England, many centuries before farming began in Britain (Schiermeier 2015). There is also evidence of goods being exchanged between Saudi Arabia, Iran and Egypt. Around 6,000 years ago, English stone axes were exported to France, while Italian polished jade ones went to England.

Then, in the Bronze Age, English copper mined 3,500 years ago was going to France, the Netherlands, Denmark and northern Germany (Williams 2019). Amber was being transported along the 'Amber Road' from northern Europe to Italy, Greece and Egypt. South East Asian islanders were taking artefacts (e.g. outriggers), crops (e.g. coconuts, bananas, sandalwood) and spices (e.g. cinnamon) to and from India and Sri Lanka (Findlay and O'Rourke 2007). There was trade too in Indian cotton, sugarcane from the Philippines, Indonesian spices, Malaysian tin and tea from China.

There may be other explanations for such widespread movements of goods, but trade seems the most likely. That is particularly true when one considers the high value of some of these goods to many people – obsidian tools, jade axes and exotic spices for example – making them highly prized in trade.

Records and recriminations

We can see just how strong commercial relationships were in the ancient world from 4,500-year-old records found at Deir el-Medina in Egypt (McDowell 1999). They show that workers on the pyramids had their own money-barter trading system. Goods were priced in a fixed quantity of grain, silver or copper, the *deben*. Thus, a jar of fresh fat priced at 15 copper *deben* might be exchanged for three tunics at 5 *deben* each or five baskets at 3 *deben* each. It was rare for physical quantities of grain, silver or copper actually to be used in transactions: the *deben* served mainly as the unit of account. But this enabled the Egyptian workers to overcome the inherent problem of barter systems – that one side might not have anything to exchange that the other side wanted (think hungry barbers searching for bakers who need haircuts). Instead, one side would supply the goods and keep an account book showing how many *deben* the other owed.

Services too were traded: for example, there were high-ly developed arrangements for leasing out donkeys (the ancient equivalent of van hire). And like today, there were also complaints: 'He brought me a donkey, but I returned it to him; and he brought me this other one, but it is not good either ... let him bring me a good donkey or else my money' wrote one angry worker. Nor is this the only complaint known from the ancient world: in Babylon around 3,750 years ago, a customer wrote to a merchant called Ea-nasir complaining of poor quality copper and of the rough treatment of the servant who handled the business. Ea-nasir, who imported copper from the Persian Gulf into Mesopotamia (modern-day Iraq), filed the complaint at home – alongside the many others that he had received.

Gift exchange and the money revolution

Most trade in the ancient world was 'gift exchange' – not people exchanging goods for money, but people exchanging goods for other goods (Selkirk 2020). Indeed, some goods, such as the huge quantities of elaborate metalwork and jewellery produced in Minoan Crete 4,000 years ago, seem to have been produced specifically for trading.

But it was the invention of money, around 2,500 years ago, that revolutionised trade, turning gift or barter trade into the market economy. Hugely more efficient, this innovation boosted not just wealth and luxury (such as spices imported from India and China and vast strides in art, architecture and culture) but independence too – since, using money, almost everyone could trade for their personal benefit. And ultimately, that gave rise to democracy (Selkirk 2020).

Suddenly, the Mediterranean economies took off. Rome grew rich on the sale of grain and wine, allowing it to create a military and trading empire over much of Europe and North Africa. Everyday goods from Italy, and polished red Samian ware from France, were exported as far as Hadrian's Wall in northern England, the northernmost extremity of the Roman Empire. Even more impressively, the Silk Road was opening up, allowing goods from the Mediterranean to be sent to Antioch in Syria, across Mesopotamia, eastward through the Zagros Mountains to Ecbatana (modern Iran) and Merv (Turkmenistan), then on to Afghanistan, Mongolia and China. And of course Asian products flowed in the opposite direction. China began to trade, by sea as well as land, with Java, Sumatra, Vietnam, South Asia and out to the Red Sea. India and Sri Lanka, well placed to be intermediaries, traded Chinese goods on to Rome and sent luxuries such as frankincense back to China. And so it went on.

Medieval trading routes

These few examples show how surprisingly extensive trade was in prehistoric and ancient times. It would become even more so. By the year 1000, for example, the Islamic world (mainly North Africa, the Persian Gulf, Mesopotamia and Iran) had links to every known region of the globe. Its brokers settled in places as distant as China. Its merchants exchanged salt and textiles for West African gold and traded by land and sea with India and South East Asia. It sent pepper, spices, textiles and silver to Europe, horses to India, and gold and spices further east. Eastern Europe sent China slaves, furs and silver and got Chinese paper from merchants in Central Asia and perfumes from South East Asia – which in turn sold sandalwood to East Asia and rice and gemstones to South Asia. East Asia, meanwhile, sold porcelain to the Mediterranean, tea to Central Asia and copper to South East Asia – an endless web of international trade (Findlay and O'Rourke 2007).

Western Europe adopted money early on, allowing thirteenth-century Venice, originally a swamp on the northeast coast of Italy, to grow rich by facilitating trade between western Europe, the Islamic world and China. The Venetian merchant and explorer Marco Polo travelled through Asia along the Silk Road between 1271 and 1295, becoming a celebrity for his writings about the exotic cultures he encountered. Venice monopolised the spice trade, while Genoa, on Italy's northwest coast, exploited its proximity to Spain, Portugal and France.

New ideas and new worlds

Ideas and technologies flowed too. The Arabic number system replaced the more cumbersome Roman version. Commerce became based on writing and record-keeping, contributing to the spread of literacy. The needs of trade advanced female literacy in particular – when merchants were at sea, they needed literate family members to keep their businesses running. With literacy came greater independence, the questioning of received opinions, and the advancement of science and the arts that would become essential parts of the European Renaissance.

> In a world where every society and every civilization has borrowed heavily from the cultures of other societies and other civilizations, everyone does not have to go back to square one and discover fire and the wheel for [themselves] ... Europeans did not have to continue copying scrolls by hand after the Chinese invented paper and printing. Malaysia could become the world's leading rubber-producing nation after planting seeds taken from Brazil.
>
> — Thomas Sowell (2002)

Europe's trading relations would expand again with the discovery of the Americas by Christopher Columbus in 1492, opening up the New World, and by Vasco de Gama's discovery, six years later, of the sea passage to India around the Cape of Good Hope, allowing direct trade with South East and East Asia, and breaking the Venetian–Islamic stranglehold on spices (the price of pepper fell by four-fifths).

Adam Smith (1776) would later describe these discoveries as 'the two most important events recorded in the history of mankind,' enabling distant peoples to 'relieve one another's wants, to increase one another's enjoyments, and to encourage one another's industry.' Yet he was equally dismayed that the new maritime routes also increased the opportunities for powerful European nations to exploit other lands and peoples.

3   THE RISE OF INTERNATIONAL TRADE

The mercantilist era

When Adam Smith was writing, the dominant view of world trade was *mercantilism*. This was the view that a country's wealth was measured, not by its productive output – the Gross National Product (GNP) we use today – but by the volume of natural resources, especially gold and silver, that it could amass. Imports coming from abroad were therefore seen as bad because it meant that gold and silver had to be given up in order to pay for them. Exports were seen as good because these precious metals came back. Trade was 'zero-sum' – the world's wealth was fixed, so only sellers could benefit from trade, never buyers. One nation could get rich only by making others poorer (Butler 2007). Based on this thinking, a vast edifice of controls was erected – taxes on imports, subsidies to exporters and protections for domestic industries.

From the sixteenth to the eighteenth centuries, the mercantilist view drove the maritime nations of France, Britain, Spain, Portugal and the Netherlands to build empires and to claim and colonise as many lands as they could, in pursuit of commodities they could sell for gold and silver – and in pursuit of those precious metals themselves.

Thus, Spain colonised Central and much of South America, crushing the Inca civilisation of Peru, the Maya of Central America and the Aztecs of Mexico as they plundered territory, gold and silver; Portugal established colonies in Brazil, sub-Saharan Africa, India, China and Japan; Britain and France occupied North America and many other regions of the world; the Netherlands colonised South Africa and Indonesia. There were bitter rivalries and conflicts as these competing empires vied to exploit distant places and protect their trading routes to them.

Enriched by their diverse acquisitions, these empires brought all kinds of goods to Europe, some already available but rare and expensive, some new and exotic, some commonplace: among them tea, coffee, sugar, rum, spices, tobacco, potatoes, rice, cotton, calico, silk, furs, porcelain, lumber and iron (Hartley 2008).

But while maritime expansion boosted mutually beneficial trade between willing participants in distant lands, it also expanded the ability of Europe's imperial and colonial powers to exploit resources and populations across the globe. Much of what passed for 'free trade' in fact took place at the point of a gun. Thus, Britain's East India Company, though nominally a trading concern, was given royal authority to use military force to fight rival traders. In 1757 it seized the entire Mughal state of Bengal – the first of many forcible annexations – levying taxes and customs duties, which it used to buy and export Indian goods to Britain. Adam Smith, the strongest advocate of genuine free trade and its benefits, roundly condemned the European empires for such exploitation, and for using their superior might to 'commit with impunity every sort of injustice in those remote countries' (Smith 1776).

It was mercantilism, not free trade, that promoted imperialism, which in turn promoted colonialism. And colonialism promoted another perversion of free trade, namely slavery. Thus, from Portugal's possessions in West Africa, Africans were sold as domestic servants in Europe and as slaves on sugar plantations in Portuguese-held Madeira and Cape Verde. British slavers engaged in a 'triangular trade', taking manufactures to Africa in exchange for slaves whom they transported to labour in colonial plantations in the Caribbean, then taking the resulting sugar and tobacco crops back to Britain. Smith again condemned the 'brutality and baseness' of this 'miserable' subjection of 'nations of heroes' by European 'wretches' (Smith 1759, 1763, 1776). To him, as to many of his contemporaries and to us today, it was not only morally contemptible but a perversion of the whole idea of legitimate free trade.

Faltering moves towards free trade

In *The Wealth of Nations*, his broadside against mercantilism, Adam Smith argued that legitimate trade – not that which is forced on anyone – is best left genuinely free (Smith 1776). The vast edifice of mercantilist controls (and the evils of imperialism and colonialism that it bred) was a mistake. He reasoned that if an exchange was genuinely voluntary, it must benefit both sides, since neither side would willingly enter a bargain if they expected to lose from it. Sellers profit from the deal by getting cash, but buyers profit too by getting the goods they want. Imports are just as valuable to us as our exports are to others. When we agree to trade, we each deliver value to the other. Wealth is not fixed but is *created* by trade. We do not have to make our customers poorer in order to make ourselves richer: we can each grow richer by embracing mutual free trade – the policy of allowing goods and services to be traded between countries with as few restrictions as possible.

As if to illustrate the point, just a few months after Smith's book was published in 1776, Britain's relationship with its North American colonists descended into open conflict. True to mercantilist principles, Britain had attempted to reserve all trade with the colonies to itself, forbidding them to trade with others. Its attempt to impose new taxes on the colonists was the last straw: they took up arms and made themselves into an independent country.

But mercantilist notions persisted, even in the new country. The first major law to be passed under the new Constitution of the United States was the 1789 Tariff Act. Designed to raise revenue and protect US manufacturing against cheaper European imports, it imposed duties of up to 50 per cent on imported goods, including steel, ships and textiles. Thomas Jefferson opposed such high tariffs, fearing retaliation against American rice, tobacco and cotton exports; yet as President, facing trade disruptions arising from Britain's wars against Napoleon, Jefferson himself in 1807 introduced an embargo on exports, and then a strict no-trade policy against Britain. It proved costly and damaging to both sides and culminated in the War of 1812.

Farewell to the Corn Laws

Britain too pursued mercantilist protections. With peace eventually restored, world prices of grain (including wheat, oats and barley) fell markedly. To protect its own producers, Britain introduced the 'Corn Laws' – restrictions designed to keep out cheaper grain imports. But while that benefited landowners (a dominant force in Parliament), it kept basic food prices high for ordinary workers. Shortages due to bad harvests in 1816 led to serious rioting.

Opponents of the restrictions formed the Anti-Corn Law League. Led by manufacturer Richard Cobden and leading free-trade advocate John Bright (both later Members of Parliament), the League argued that repeal would end the unjust returns of landlords, eradicate rural poverty, give workers more regular employment and promote trade, which in turn would promote peace between nations (Butler 2019).

> I see in the Free-trade principle that which shall act on the moral world as the principle of gravitation in the universe – drawing men together, thrusting aside the antagonism of race, and creed, and language, and uniting us in the bonds of eternal peace.
>
> — Richard Cobden (1846)

However, it would take yet more crop failures before the Corn Laws were repealed. In 1845, potato blight in Ireland started to cause huge food shortages and famine. Though his Conservative Party traditionally favoured landowners,

Prime Minister Sir Robert Peel moved to repeal the restrictions. His fellow Conservative, the Duke of Wellington, persuaded the House of Lords to agree – if only to stave off the threat of insurrection, rather than any commitment to free trade.

An era of more open trade

The 1846 repeal of the Corn Laws led to rapid falls in grain prices. By 1900, when new railways and steamships were bringing Britain abundant grain from the vast American prairies, its price was a tenth of earlier levels (O'Rourke 1999). Imported food meant that Britain's farmland became less valuable, its price falling by nearly 40 per cent (O'Rourke 1997). A few rich landowners lost out, but many less-well-off British consumers gained.

Manufacturing benefited from trade too. As well as steam transport, the telegraph (and later the telephone) brought European manufacturers closer to suppliers and customers in their colonies and ex-colonies. Fruit, vegetables and other products could now be traded quickly over long distances. Trading ports expanded in the Americas, Africa and Asia, as did the new merchant class, with tens of millions of people migrating to seek their fortune in the emerging colonial markets (Poon and Rigby 2017).

The *centre* of trade remained Europe: it led manufacturing, and there were millions of consumers to be supplied. But the *focus* of trade shifted westwards. Britain, for example, imported American cotton (a much stronger fibre than traditional wool), using water and steam power to make cheap fabrics and finished clothes for export to all parts of the world. It was a revolution not just for industry but for the lives of working people in countries all round the world – albeit one built partly on the forced labour of other, enslaved workers in the plantations of America.

The decline of free trade policies

Yet the outbreak of World War I in Europe in 1914 marked the end of almost a century of relatively free trade. The war brought a new kind of mercantilism. Its objective was not to earn precious metals by boosting exports and restricting imports, but to amass the raw materials and manufactures needed to wage war – and prevent enemies from doing the same thing. This idea saw countries restricting their exports and increasing their imports while blockading others' exports to enemy countries. New technologies were applied to this end – mines, submarines, even aerial bombing, along with blacklisting firms who exported goods to enemies (Findlay and O'Rourke 2007).

Even after the war ended in 1918, the mercantilist mentality lingered. The victorious powers did not want their defeated enemies to prosper through unrestricted trade, and possibly build up materials that could be used for war again. They also wanted to protect their own jobs and industries. And their centralised wartime control systems made it easier for them to continue intervening. But the economic costs were high. International trade, which had grown steadily to a peak of 13 per cent of world output in

1913, was down to 10 per cent by 1921, and just 5 per cent by 1935 – no more than it had been in the 1840s. Indeed, it would be the mid 1970s before trade would match its 1913 share of output again.

Worsening economic conditions in America merely prompted yet more restrictions. In the 1928 US presidential election, Herbert Hoover promised measures to protect farm workers, and the 1929 US stock market crash made the calls for trade barriers still louder. In 1928, the Smoot–Hawley Tariff Act, which would impose duties on over 20,000 imported goods, was introduced into Congress. When it was passed in 1930, America's trading partners, led by Canada, retaliated with their own import controls, deepening the economic slowdown (that would turn into the Great Depression) even more.

By 1933, American outputs and incomes had almost halved. These effects were felt globally too, particularly in Europe, where they fed a militaristic nationalism. As the European nations braced themselves for what would become World War II, the idea of free trade seemed a thing of the past. It would return, but not for a long time and not without concerted international effort.

PART TWO

THE PRINCIPLES OF TRADE

4 THE THEORY OF TRADE

Exchange and value

Adam Smith's description of voluntary exchange as ben-
efiting both sides, not only the side receiving payment,
was devastating for mercantilism. At the time, though, it
seemed puzzling: after all, the two sides are exchanging
the same good, at the same price, so how can one expect
to benefit by acquiring it, and the other expect to benefit
by giving it up? Doesn't it mean that one or the other must
be wrong about the value of the item, and must therefore
actually lose from the exchange?

The answer is no, because, as Smith realised, value does
not exist in goods themselves but in the minds of their be-
holders. When people exchange goods, they do so because
they each value the same good differently. A child, for example, may happily swap with a schoolmate some toy they
are bored with in return for a much cheaper toy that they
find more amusing. The swap goes ahead only if the other
child values the toys the opposite way around. Interesting-
ly, nothing new is created through the exchange – no *new*
toys have been made – yet both sides have benefited. Value
has been increased (Butler 2011).

The same is true where goods or services are traded for money. Customers today in Smith's chilly homeland willingly buy bananas grown by farmers in sunny Colombia because they value the fruit more than the money they hand over in exchange. The Colombian farmers, conversely, value the money more than the fruit. That is because, in Colombia's tropical climate and with their specialist farming knowledge, they can produce, very cheaply, far more bananas than they and their families could possibly eat. Then, they can sell their surplus to people who cannot easily grow bananas, and buy something more valuable to them with the proceeds.

Specialisation

This point takes us to Smith's other insight: that through specialising – what he called the *division of labour* – people are able to produce far, far more than they need for their own use. Specialisation allows them to build up surpluses that they can then trade.

Smith's famous example of division of labour in action was a pin factory. Most of us would be hard pressed to make a single neat pin in a day, even if the metal were already smelted for us. Yet the ten people in the pin factory that Smith visited could make 48,000 pins in a day because they each specialised in different parts of the operation and had acquired the specialist tools that they needed to do it (Butler 2011). One, he says, 'draws out the wire, another straights it, a third cuts it, a fourth points it, a fifth grinds it at the top for receiving the head.' In total, around eighteen distinct specialist operations were involved (Smith 1776).

Trade exists largely because of the specialisation that enables people to make more than they need, exchanging their surplus for things they value more. But the fact that exchange is possible also *encourages* such specialisation by providing the mechanism by which people can benefit from producing a surplus. Put simply, it pays to produce, and then trade, what you can produce cheaply, easily and well.

Comparative advantage

As Smith again pointed out, there is no point in a household trying to become self-sufficient, producing everything they need such as food, shoes or clothing, when they can buy better and cheaper products from other people who specialise in producing them. And what is true of individual households is also true of nations (Smith 1776). Why try to grow grapes and make wine in chilly Scotland, when it can be produced at a thirtieth of the cost in balmy France?

Likewise, it is certainly possible to grow bananas in Britain, but growers would need to build large and costly glasshouses and install energy-guzzling heaters in order to grow them on any scale. It is very much cheaper for people in Britain to buy bananas from Colombia, where they can be grown easily, abundantly and cheaply. In terms of growing bananas, Colombia has an *absolute advantage* over Britain. But, with its more industrial economy, Britain is better at making medicines and machinery, which it exports to Colombia. Both countries benefit from this exchange.

> If a foreign country can supply us with a commodity cheaper than we ourselves can make it, better buy it of them with some part of the produce of our own industry, employed in a way in which we have some advantage.
>
> — Adam Smith (1776)

This idea was further refined by another British economist, David Ricardo (1817). With his concept of *comparative advantage*, he explained that it makes sense for a country to trade, even if they are better at *everything* than others. A country should focus on what it does better *in comparison* to its trading partners. For instance, even if Colombia could produce machinery cheaper and better than other countries, it might still make more money by producing bananas, because it is so very much better at that than most other countries. And by specialising in growing bananas, it can make itself better still: it can increase the scale and efficiency of its production and invest in whatever is needed – such as fertilisers, pest control, plant breeding, harvesting and packing technologies – to supply *even better and cheaper* bananas.

Or to illustrate the point with a more everyday example: a doctor might have better keyboard and telephone skills than the clinic receptionist; but it still makes sense for the doctor to focus on diagnosing and treating patients, rather than spend valuable time typing the practice letters and answering the phone.

Unequal advantages and trade

While Ricardo himself proposed specialisation on the basis of how much *labour* it took for different countries to produce the same product, other factors such as land and capital are also important for manufacturing. And again, these resources are not evenly distributed between countries. Britain, for example, has more capital and more skilled labour than Colombia; Colombia has a lot of unskilled labour but better conditions for growing fruit.

Thoughts such as these led two twentieth-century Swedish economists, Eli Heckscher and Bertil Ohlin, to suggest that international patterns of production and trade could be predicted on the basis of what *factor endowments* – the various resources you need to produce particular things – were abundant and cheap, or scarce and expensive, in different countries (Ohlin 1933).

Their original *Heckscher–Ohlin model* focused only on countries' different endowments of labour and capital. But later economists broadened it to include other relevant differences such as location and climate. For example, a verdant tropical country like Colombia may have an advantage in producing fruit; while Ireland's moderate, moist climate and lush meadows give it an advantage in raising dairy cows and producing butter and cheese. America's technical expertise gives it an advantage in designing and building aircraft, while China's abundance of cheap labour gives it an advantage in assembling electronic equipment. In this way, trade compensates for the unequal distribution of resources in different countries.

Who trades with whom?

Plainly, countries with very different resource allocations – warm or cold, skilled or unskilled, coastal or landlocked, fertile or barren – have much to gain from trading with each other. But quite similar countries also trade: there are large volumes of trade between the US and Canada, for example, or between the countries of Europe; and there are growing volumes within South America or South East Asia too.

Yet this demonstrates how very advanced world trade, and the exploitation of comparative advantage, has become. Countries that appear similar in terms of wealth or location or natural resources can still find an edge in supplying some particular good and trading it with the others. For instance, Sri Lanka is only 35 miles from India, but supplies it with processed meat, spices, rubber tyres, insulation and gloves. India, meanwhile, supplies Sri Lanka with minerals, cereals, cotton and machinery. Likewise, Britain imports food from other European countries but exports services back to them. Vietnam exports minerals, fabric and plastics to neighbouring Cambodia, which in turn supplies Vietnam with fruit, vegetables, rubber and wood products. Each exploits its slight edge over neighbours, and trade keeps pushing them to maintain and improve that edge.

Comparative advantage may be more obvious when trade is between different countries. But it is a feature of domestic commerce within individual countries too. For example, New York sells financial services to the rest of the

US, while the Midwest supplies manufactures and grains, and California sells fruit and wine. There are also noteworthy *clusters* of activities within countries – Hyderabad in India is a major IT centre, as is Silicon Valley in California.

Defying gravity?

Trade between similar countries may simply reflect the fact that they are close, perhaps even sharing a similar language, stage of development or similar cultural, legal or financial institutions. Indeed, the *gravity model* of trade suggests that the volume of trade between two countries depends largely on their proximity and the size of their economies.

There is some evidence that this is true, even in modern service-based trade (such as banking, insurance and consultancy). Whether it will remain so in a globalised world is an open question. With ever-cheaper transportation, greater standardisation in customs procedures, efficiency-boosting IT in logistics, better communications and much else, trade with distant nations is becoming easier and easier.

5 THE BENEFITS OF TRADE

Trade, then, benefits both sides and would not happen if it did not. The obvious benefits, which economists call the *static gains from trade*, are the increase in value that comes from voluntary exchange, raising public welfare (particularly that of consumers) and boosting economic growth. But trade also sets off events that *accelerate* growth and economic development, known as the *dynamic gains from trade*. And there are non-economic benefits, *non-material gains from trade*, too.

Static gains from trade

Greater incomes. Trade delivers higher national income. The rolling back of mercantilist trading barriers was a large part of Britain's economic boom in the late nineteenth century (Cain 1982). Similarly, the post-war efforts to encourage trade increased the incomes of Western nations in the late twentieth century (Terborgh 2003). More recently, South Asia and China/South East Asia entering into the global trading networks in the 1980s and 1990s set off the 'Asian Miracle' that has taken nearly a billion people out of dire poverty (World Bank 2016).

Research suggests that each 1 per cent growth in trade increases the incomes of a country's citizens by about 2 per cent (Frankel and Romer 1999). It has enriched even countries with few natural resources. The major trading centres of Hong Kong and Singapore, for instance, were relatively poor places at the end of World War II but are now among the richest. By contrast, countries with plentiful natural resources that cut themselves off from trade, such as North Korea, rank low on world prosperity tables.

Choice, quality, value and welfare. Trade delivers more than higher income alone, however. It also delivers a better quality of life. Plainly, richer countries can afford to spend more on things like education, better healthcare and a cleaner environment. But these and other quality-of-life benefits are also promoted through new ideas, practices and processes coming from abroad.

Trade also gives consumers access to a vast array of products from around the world, increasing the choice, quality and value available to them. No longer are they limited to local products. They can enjoy the products of other lands and cultures, including different kinds of textiles, clothing and footwear, or foods and cuisine, or electronics, or vehicles, or household goods, even services such as banking or education or repairs. Producers too can import the world's best manufacturing equipment to help raise their own productivity.

Liberal values. The fact that trade is associated with growth and rising prosperity does not necessarily mean that it *causes* them, though it certainly helps. Perhaps the attitudes that support trade – including liberal values such as the respect for others' rights, toleration, peace, the rule of law, a free economy and a free society – are the main drivers (Butler 2013). Historically, societies have advanced most rapidly where these values have prevailed and where the institutions that preserve them (such as representative democracy and an impartial justice system) are well maintained.

Dynamic gains from trade

Specialisation and productivity. As mentioned in chapter 4, the specialisation on which trade is based can lead to huge increases in productivity. It also promotes the better use of resources (such as land, labour, materials and capital) because it pushes producers to extract greater output from the same inputs. For example, it encourages them to seek out *economies of scale* (such as larger and more efficient factories), *economies of scope* (like supermarkets selling clothes and household items alongside groceries), and *economies of agglomeration* (such as the clustering of IT firms in Silicon Valley). In addition, the wider market that trade brings also promotes the better use of a country's resources. For example, a non-trading country might have large expanses of idle land; with trade, these might be developed to produce export crops that benefit foreign consumers and bring cash for domestic producers.

Switching resources. The fact that specialisation and trade are so beneficial encourages people to move from low-value employment into more productive industries where they have a comparative advantage. The workers who once toiled in small farm terraces on the stony, sun-scorched hillsides of the Greek islands, for instance, now work in the hotels, restaurants and shops that serve tourists drawn by the same rugged landscape that makes farming so unprofitable. In the tourist sector, they earn more – and buy their food from more efficient farmers in other communities and countries.

Infrastructure and investment. The infrastructure and investment needed to bring goods to their customers (such as ports, airports, roads, tunnels, bridges, as well as networks, accounting systems, financial instruments and even legal arrangements) can of course be used by other traders – reducing their costs and enabling them to reach new markets. The gain is dynamic, because infrastructure and investment deliver similar benefits to future businesses, which may be trading products as yet unimagined.

Competition, innovation and progress. International trade greatly widens the pool of talent involved in supplying products to markets. Such increased competition means domestic producers have to make their own activities more cost-effective, or risk losing business to outsiders. They have to control costs and cut waste. They must stay sharp in order to understand what customers want and how those wants can be satisfied, and to anticipate future trends on both fronts. They need to keep trying new things, to innovate and improve both their offer to customers and their own production processes. And this constant pressure to innovate and improve in turn drives progress (Ridley 2020).

> The message is so blatantly obvious from history that free trade causes mutual prosperity while protectionism causes poverty that it seems incredible that anybody ever thinks otherwise. There is not a single example of a country opening its borders to trade and ending up poorer...
>
> — Matt Ridley (2010)

Non-material benefits

As Richard Cobden realised, the non-material, non-economic benefits of trade are also profound (Cobden 1846). Regardless of their economic impact, the choice, innovation and progress that are brought by trade improve our lives and the world we live in. Trade brings us better clothing, a better diet, better healthcare, better technology and much else.

Peace, which is not only valuable in its own right but also essential to economic life, is also promoted by trade, because trade demands that we deal with people from outside our own country and culture. To trade well with others, we must come to understand – and respect, or at least tolerate – their values. Such familiarity diminishes any hostility we may have towards them.

The benefit that trade brings to both sides is good reason for nations to resolve their differences peacefully rather than militarily. When we are dependent on others for many of the essential goods we need, it pays to cooperate with them and keep those goods flowing. And the more that we are invested in trade, the greater the incentive for us to preserve the peace. Trading nations simply have more to lose from military conflicts that disrupt supply networks or threaten production. Trade makes it less likely that conflicts will escalate into open hostilities. As a remark attributed (probably wrongly) to the nineteenth-century French political economist Frédéric Bastiat put it: 'If goods do not cross borders, armies will.'

Importers and exporters in particular need to understand their customers and their customers' values and institutions. They may even need to master the other's language – a source of great insight into how its speakers think. Consumers too, noting the diverse origins of the imports that they buy each day, may also come to appreciate the values of other peoples and other cultures. The international nature of today's entertainment (e.g. movies and TV) provides an example of how extensively trade has already exposed us to other cultures and ways of life.

PART THREE

DOUBTS ABOUT TRADE

6 WINNERS AND LOSERS IN TRADE

Economic change creates winners and losers

While nearly all economists agree on the general benefits of free trade, trade inevitably produces losers as well as winners.

In this, trade is no different from any other part of economic life. On the plus side, economic competition stimulates innovation, invention and improvement in the things we produce and how we produce them. That delivers progress which boosts the welfare and prosperity of humanity in general. But economic change inevitably disrupts the lives of some people, especially those whose own industries are made redundant by it.

Thus the coming of motor vehicles ruined the businesses of livery stables; then Henry Ford's production-line system made hand-built cars uneconomic. Digital cameras made film cameras largely obsolete; the incorporation of cameras into smartphones did the same for them. Few people today would want to go back to horse transport or film cameras, or any other outdated technology, but each development displaces those who work in them.

As well as changes in technology, changes in consumer tastes create winners and losers too. Today's more casual choices in dress, for example, have seen traditional shoe-makers eclipsed by sports shoe manufacturers such as Nike and Reebok; while the 'fast fashion' trend has seen low-cost transnational retailers such as Zara, H&M, Primark, Uniqlo and Gap prosper at the expense of traditional local clothes shops. And in many countries, environmental concerns have prompted customers to switch away from plastics and fossil fuels, causing problems for producers who use or supply them.

Natural events can disrupt industries too. The Covid-19 pandemic, for example, led to the widespread closure of restaurants, cinemas and shops in many countries – though takeaways, digital entertainment companies and online retailers boomed.

Change, then, brings winners and losers, though it is a part of life. And a significant source of change – opening up economies to new ideas, new technologies, new products and new lifestyles – is trade.

Dislocation in richer countries

A prominent example of the constant change wrought by trade is the outsourcing of manufacturing jobs from richer countries to lower-cost ones. Manufacturing workers then lose their jobs and struggle to find others. Sometimes, whole areas once dominated by particular industries, such as the north of England (coal, steel) and the American Midwest (steel, car making) become 'de-industrialised', causing deep social deprivation. And as businesses refocus on their global operations and invest less at home, opportunities and community support both diminish (Hochberg 2020: ch. 2).

There is some evidence that this leads to a rise in earnings inequalities (Poon and Rigby 2017: ch. 6). But while some people lose their jobs, trade creates winners too: it increases choice for consumers and makes products cheaper. One US estimate suggests that each 1 per cent increase in imports reduces prices by 2.4 per cent (Hausman and Leibtag 2005). That includes the prices of essentials such as food, clothing and footwear, which helps poorer citizens in particular and may offset any rise in income inequalities.

Also, while some manufacturing job losses are due to global outsourcing and cheaper imports, trade cannot be blamed for them all. True, richer countries have seen a decline in manufacturing employment – down from a 1979 peak of 19.4 million in America, for example, to just 12.5 million today. But research suggests that around 85 per cent of that decline stems from productivity improvements such as automation, IT and logistics, rather than trade – improvements that may well have happened naturally, without trade (Klein 2016; see also Devaraj et al. 2017; Hicks and Devaraj 2015).

International trade may also have created new opportunities in rich countries, such as in high-value or advanced manufacturing (Klein 2016). Many displaced industrial workers and their families will also find jobs in more productive and competitive sectors such as healthcare, education, retail, services or IT. Over a third of Americans in manufacturing find a new job within five weeks, and two thirds within fourteen weeks (US Bureau of Labor

Statistics 2020). And though factories may crumble and machinery rust, the capital that counts in the 'people economy' of today is *human capital*, the abilities and experience of individuals themselves (Pirie 2002), and the networks that enable them to work together (Butler 2018).

Labour productivity

Despite all this, people in richer countries often believe that competition from cheap labour countries is unfair. Producers complain that they have to pay minimum wages and taxes that are many times higher than those paid by their foreign competitors. Workers worry that their jobs will be lost because of customers switching from domestic-made goods to cheaper foreign-made ones.

But changes that bring problems to some may be a boon to others. Developing countries have a comparative advantage in labour costs. Outsourcing tasks to them allows richer-country manufacturers to reduce prices for their customers. It also spurs them to focus on their own comparative advantages – tasks requiring higher skills or a lot of capital equipment, say.

In Mexico, for example, wages are much lower than those in the US, which is why many manufacturing jobs have been relocated there. But the real shift is probably much less. Mexican workers are less productive than American workers, because they have less capital to help them work efficiently. Since it takes more capital-poor Mexicans to do the same job that one capital-rich American could do, the rise in new manufacturing jobs in Mexico does not mean that an equivalent number have been lost in America.

Change and globalisation

Usually, economic changes happen slowly. Even in wealthy countries, horse transport was still in use fifty years after motor vehicles arrived. Such gradual changes give businesses time to adjust to the new reality and enable workers to find more productive new jobs.

However, critics of trade worry that the world's increasing specialisation may expose individuals, businesses, countries and indeed the world to more sudden, widespread disruptions. When vital products come from abroad, there is always the risk that their supply might be disrupted, accidentally or deliberately.

The Napoleonic Wars, for example, disrupted Britain's trade with the US. They also ruined France's textile industry, since producers could no longer access Caribbean cotton (Krpec and Hodulak 2019). The 1973 oil embargo by the Organization of Petroleum Exporting Countries (OPEC) seriously damaged heavy industry in Britain, Japan, the US and Canada. And even more recently, in the Covid-19 pandemic, many countries found that the personal protective equipment (PPE) they needed for hospital staff was mostly imported, and that they were competing with other nations for supplies.

Exposure to competition

Countries face particular disruption when they have shielded their industries behind trade barriers for years or decades, and then these protections are suddenly swept away. For example, their governments may enter into 'free trade agreements' (FTAs) that reduce trading restrictions between them, welcoming the overall gains of that but leaving once-protected industries unable to compete. Indeed, the sudden influx of cheaper foreign imports may spell ruin for entire sectors.

> People say free trade causes dislocation. In actual fact, it's
> the lowering of trade barriers that causes the dislocation.
> — P. J. O'Rourke (2009)

Naturally, the industries that feel most threatened by international trade are those that lobby hardest against opening their markets to competitors. But the privileged protection they have gained has come at the expense of consumers, in terms of less choice, higher prices and poorer quality. At some point, they must adjust to reality.

Sadly, that adjustment can take a long time, during which there are losses to these industries, their workers and the country in general. This is perhaps the most common criticism of globalisation, and to the WTO's ambition to reduce trade barriers as rapidly as possible. It is for this reason that critics of globalisation argue that industries in poorer countries may need continued protection until they can become large and cost-effective enough to compete on world markets – the so-called 'infant industry' argument (see chapter 9).

7 CONCERNS ABOUT GLOBALISATION

Coercion of poorer countries

Globalisation's harshest critics see it as a cynical strategy of richer countries to exploit poorer ones by undercutting local producers. They argue that richer countries dominate the WTO and set its rules, forcing poorer countries to lower their trade barriers, while cynically preserving their own.

But while richer nations have more economic leverage, they do not necessarily have more political leverage in international discussions. (If anything, the large falls in manufacturing tariffs negotiated during the early GATT years benefited developing countries most, though they gave few concessions in return.) WTO agreements must be accepted by all members before they can be enacted, so countries can block proposals if they have reservations. And since the WTO now has 164 members, most countries presumably think that, on balance, trade agreements generally benefit them.

Perpetual lag?

Some critics still argue that, whatever its benefits, trade does not change the unequal relationship between rich and poor countries. The so-called Prebisch–Singer thesis suggested that, as the world grew wealthier, the demand for manufactured goods would grow faster than the demand for primary goods such as food, oil and minerals. (Quite simply, a wealthier world buys more luxuries, but there is a limit to the amount of food or fuel that even the richest people can consume.) Since richer countries produce manufactures and poorer ones produce mainly primary goods, the latter will always lag behind.

However, this idea, popular in the 1960s and 1970s, is no longer tenable. The prices of primary goods are volatile, being hit by financial crises, manufacturing downturns and natural disasters, but they surge during global booms. They soared in the early 2000s, for example, due to rising demand from China and other fast-growing emerging markets. Meanwhile, under the pressure of competition, the prices of manufactures have fallen steadily – some (such as electronics, clothes and footwear) spectacularly so. Much of the production of such manufactures has now moved to poorer countries, making them less reliant on primary goods exports anyway. The most obvious conclusion from the data is that there is no lag, and not even any clear trend (*The Economist* 2020). Developing countries are not condemned to perpetual catching-up; indeed, some have grown remarkably fast.

A variant of the 'lag' argument is that trade simply reinforces colonial patterns of unequal exchange. Even today, for example, Britain has important trading links with India, Australasia and America; France with West Africa and the Caribbean; Spain with South America.

But trade is built on trust. It is easier to trust people who share your language and history. And it is harder to build links with new trading partners than simply to carry on with old ones. Even so, developing countries can and do establish new trading networks and build up their own manufacturing industries too. Indeed, exports of manufactures have overtaken exports of commodities in most developing countries outside sub-Saharan Africa. Once poor countries, such as Japan, Singapore, South Korea and China, are now major global manufacturing exporters, and are becoming major services exporters. Some former colonies are now richer than their one-time rulers. So, the idea that poorer countries will always lag behind richer ones appears mistaken.

Import substitution

Nevertheless, in the 1960s and 1970s, these ideas caused many developing countries to adopt a new policy of 'import substitution'. Their aim was to reduce their dependence on developed countries by making their own economies self-sufficient. Governments created new manufacturing industries, making steel, cars, domestic appliances, even electronics and aircraft. These 'infant industries' were protected by trade barriers and foreign exchange controls designed to stop investment going abroad.

The results were disappointing. Money was lavished on prestige projects such as steel mills that had no comparative advantage, were distant from markets and input supplies and never became profitable. Domestic economies were not developed or sizeable enough to absorb their products. The resulting strain on government finances led to debt, inflation, low (often negative) growth rates and even falls in developing countries' share of export markets, the exact opposite of what was intended (Poon and Rigby 2017: ch. 5).

Yet some governments pursued the 'import substitution' idea even into the 1980s. Brazil, for example, tried to boost domestic computer hardware manufacture by restricting imports and hindering joint ventures with foreign manufacturers. Sadly, this left the country's other businesses paying twice the world price for equipment that was technologically out of date, hitting Brazil's competitiveness (Brooke 1990).

By contrast, developing economies in Asia grew rapidly. They did not adopt the import substitution strategy but played to their comparative advantage in low-skilled manufacturing or as traders, earning their revenues from exporting. As a result, Singapore, Hong Kong, South Korea, Japan, Taiwan and others were able to industrialise far quicker than Africa and Latin America, defying the Prebisch–Singer predictions of a permanent lag. When South Korea scrapped almost all tariffs in 1960, its economy took off, with exports growing at 30 per cent and GDP growing at 10 per cent (Krueger 2020: ch. 4). Such examples encouraged developing countries to abandon import substitution policies and instead embrace trade.

The fair trade movement

There is a widespread humanitarian concern that globalisation may drive down the earnings of farmers in poor countries, by exposing them to competition from more efficient producers abroad. This concern, made more urgent by falls in coffee prices, led to religious and activist groups creating the Fairtrade Foundation in 1992. Its aim was to create a brand that would appeal to consumers in rich countries by guaranteeing that a greater share of the price they paid (first for coffee, but then for other products) would go to producers. The Foundation would also build long-term partnerships that would help farmers ride out volatility in prices and invest in machinery and infrastructure. On its 25th anniversary, the Foundation estimated that it had generated €1 billion in 'Fairtrade Premium' that was invested in tools, training, credit, schooling and community projects.

However worthy the Foundation's aims, some economists question whether it really promotes the long-term interests of poor farmers (Sidwell 2008). Given the size of the world coffee markets, including the billions of euros that rich countries make every year by maintaining protectionist barriers against processed coffee, €1 billion over 25 years is a relatively small sum. Moreover, much of the 'premium' goes to a small number of farmers, much of it to landowners rather than labourers, and mostly in relatively wealthy countries like Mexico. These subsidies may actually make it harder for farmers in poorer countries, like Ethiopia, to compete. Moreover, the subsidy may dampen market signals – like falling coffee prices that suggest there are too many producers – and trap farmers in their existing state, rather than prompting them to diversify and explore new products or industries. And the Foundation has eclipsed other ethical brands that may help poorer producers more effectively. The critics conclude that the fair trade movement is not a viable long-term development strategy and that equal or greater benefits can be achieved by rich countries removing tariffs on agricultural imports from poorer ones (Mohan 2010).

Exploitation of poor workers

There are concerns for industrial workers too. For example, globalisation's critics argue that transnational corporations (TNCs) force workers into 'sweatshops' with long hours, low pay and bad conditions.

The real picture is less clear (Poon and Rigby 2017). Certainly, manufacturing jobs have shifted to cheap-labour countries that tolerate lower wages, longer hours and poorer working conditions than do rich ones. But nobody is forced to work in factories making garments or electronics for export: they choose to do so because the work is safer, more secure and better paid than other options such as mining or agriculture. Their wages and hours might shock onlookers in developed countries, but are generally higher, often considerably higher, than those available in other local employments (Skarbek 2006). And higher earnings mean lower levels of child labour (Edmonds and Pavcnik 2004): factory earnings are particularly beneficial to teenage girls, allowing families to keep them in education longer and enabling them to marry and bear children later (Heath and Mobarak 2014).

Globalization ... succeeded in unifying people from around the world – against globalization. Factory workers in the United States saw their jobs being threatened by competition from China. Farmers in developing countries saw their jobs being threatened by ... crops from the United States. Workers in Europe saw hard-fought-for job protections being assailed ... Environmentalists felt that globalization undermined their decade long struggle to establish regulations to preserve our natural heritage.

— Joseph Stiglitz (2007)

Overall, the evidence shows that trade *improves* living and working standards in poorer countries. Those with high levels of foreign direct investment (FDI) have rising employment standards (Poon and Rigby 2017: ch. 6). Trade brings their citizens higher wages, more employment, reduced poverty, better nutrition, improved health and longer life (Norberg 2017). It brings workers out of the informal economy, where low wages and bad conditions are rife, and security is non-existent (McCaig and Pavcnik 2014).

Trade benefits consumers in developing countries too. Markets in food, clothing, electronics, communications, media and much else have become truly international, bringing consumers better and cheaper imported products than their local industries can supply. For the very poorest in particular, that is an important gain.

Undoubtedly, China, South East Asia, Japan, Korea, Singapore, Hong Kong or India could not have made the progress they have made without trade. Nor would the lives of many of the world's poorest people have improved so much and so quickly. For many years up to 1980, when trade started to expand rapidly, over two-fifths of the world's population lived on less than $2 a day. By 1990, that had fallen to just over a third. Now it is one in ten. And that is despite a growing world population: the 1990 poverty figure represented nearly 1.9 billion people. Given that the world population has grown by almost a third since then, we might expect $2-a-day poverty to be topping 2.5 billion by now. In fact, it is down to 500 million, mostly in sub-Saharan Africa.

Environmental concerns

Another criticism is that global trade damages the environment. Cheap-labour countries generally have lower environmental standards than richer ones; so, when manufacturing jobs are outsourced, the work is more likely to be done in factories that use fossil fuels and discharge toxic emissions. And by making agriculture more profitable, trade can lead to the over-exploitation and erosion of land, and the destruction of forests and other wildlife habitats in the search for fresh farmland.

Poorer countries respond that such complaints are hypocritical. Rich countries, they say, showed little environmental concern during their own early development: most stripped their forests for agriculture and burned fossil fuels for industry. It is unreasonable to deny developing countries the same opportunities. To do so merely prolongs the inequality between rich and poor.

Of course, the developed countries were largely unaware of the environmental impact of their earlier actions: today, nobody can ignore the potential damage. But while it is true that countries create environmental damage in their early stages of development, they get cleaner as they grow richer. As people grow wealthier, they are less willing to accept dirty factories, polluted rivers and fume-filled streets. Also, luckily, trade and growth bring us cheaper 'green' production technologies. Allowing developing countries to go rapidly through this natural cycle, therefore, will create a richer and cleaner world (Dinda 2004). In the long run, trade and growth *improve* the environment.

Another environmental concern is that global trade means goods being transported large distances, increasing the carbon footprint of what we consume. And by making production cheaper, trade encourages us to buy more products, adding to the problem (Frankel and Romer 2005).

Yet the environmental costs of transportation are lower than imagined. Containerisation and computer logistics allow goods to be shipped in bulk with amazing efficiency. Indeed, most 'food miles' are the last mile between the shop and the customer's home. In cold climates, the 'buy local' alternative of raising crops and animals locally would require more energy than importing them from warm ones.

It is wrong, therefore, to condemn trade as wholly destructive to the environment. And WTO agreements do take environmental concerns on board. The real task is to organise trade such that we protect the environment while still advancing human progress, particularly for the poorest.

Cultural imperialism

A last criticism of global trade is that it destroys local cultures, replacing them with shallow, consumerist Western lifestyles. Thus, world media are dominated by Western television, movies, social media and computer games. Instead of traditional foods, hamburgers, fried chicken, pizzas and coffee are served all round the world in branches of McDonald's, KFC, Starbucks – or local copies of them. Western stores sell Western brands in cities from Kuala Lumpur to Lima.

But cultural diffusion is nothing new. Ancient Romans read Greek philosophers in translation and imported exotic spices and fruits from afar. The Silk Road brought paper, printing and gunpowder to Europe, and new religions to China. The arrival of Indian culture in Java and Borneo fed their demand for aromatics. Arabic numbers and astronomy spread all over the world.

And cultural diffusion is a two-way process. Both sides choose and adopt what they like best from the other. America's trading partners enjoy its hamburgers (which deliver them more nutrition per dollar than most alternatives) and drink Coca-Cola (which is safe to drink everywhere, unlike many other local options). Meanwhile, Americans enjoy Chinese acupuncture, Japanese martial arts, Australian TV programmes, Scandinavian design and exotic cuisines from all round the world.

By exposing us to new ideas, trade *promotes* cultural diversity and innovation. That partly explains the growing international interest in the arts (theatre, music, architecture), local crafts, fashion, design, media (books, magazines, broadcasting, film), heritage (tourism, museums, galleries, libraries), festivals, sports and much else. Trade introduces people to different ways of living that they willingly incorporate into their own culture – if they regard it as beneficial. This two-way spread of cultures may even promote a sense of global togetherness, undermine nationalism, increase trust and promote understanding, toleration and peace (Wright 2018).

PART FOUR

PROTECTIONISM

8 PROTECTIONISM: POLITICS, TOOLS, PROBLEMS

The politics of protectionism

Given the popular concerns about the potential downsides of trade and globalisation, countries face strong pressures to discourage certain imports. In particular, they face determined lobbying from industries that fear competition from cheaper imports. While that might mean higher prices for consumers, the link is not obvious, and consumers lack the same fierce motivation. Foreign traders, meanwhile, have no votes with which to threaten domestic politicians. And once in place, controls become hard to remove – creating a protectionist ratchet.

There are many other, diverse motives behind protectionism too. Countries may wish to preserve their way of life and traditional industries such as agriculture. They might not wish to see foreign investors taking ownership of their industries. They might wish to protect new industries that are not yet large enough to compete worldwide. They might hope to raise revenues by taxing trade. Or they might even hope to silence criticism – as did China with its 200 per cent import tax on Australian wine after Australia called for an investigation into the source of Covid-19.

Protectionism is usually the product of domestic politics. For example, agriculture is a highly visible industry, which most countries see as vital to their domestic economy. Politicians therefore benefit politically from protecting it – despite the real but less visible costs that this imposes on consumers. (Worse still, each country adopts different policies to protect their agriculture. As well as being diverse, these policies can also be highly complex as they strive to deal with many different kinds of farms, owners and production methods. Agriculture, though, is often important in trade as well as domestically: around 25 per cent of US farm output is exported, for example. So, agricultural trade policies become even more complex as countries attempt to make them mesh with their diverse domestic policies. It all makes agriculture one of the most difficult topics in WTO trade negotiations.)

The tools of protectionism

Tariffs. There are also many different ways in which countries can seek to achieve protectionist ends. The most obvious are *tariffs* or customs duties – taxes on imported goods, designed to make imports less attractive to consumers, or to raise revenue, or both. Tariffs may be levied as a percentage of the value of the imported goods (*ad valorem*) or as a fixed amount on each unit, or a combination of the two.

Tariffs have been cut substantially through international action since World War II and are now widely frowned upon. But there are other, less transparent ways for a country to resist foreign imports – so-called *non-tariff barriers*.

Direct non-tariff barriers. *Quotas* or *import licences*, for example, put limits on the quantity or value of goods that can be imported into the country. They may impose an absolute restriction on how much can be imported: China, for example, puts a limit on the tonnage of rice it accepts from Cambodia. Or countries may let in a certain quantity of a good at a low or zero tariff but impose higher tariffs on any further imports. Quotas mean that domestic producers face some, but not total, competition from abroad.

But quota systems can be highly complex, making them less transparent than tariffs, potentially fuelling corruption. Also, they still raise prices for consumers. And they may prevent producers from getting the inputs they need for their business: with tariffs, inputs from abroad simply become more expensive, but with quotas, they may be impossible to get at all. That may limit the output of successful businesses and discourage new ones from setting up (Krueger 2020: ch. 5).

Another option is *voluntary export restraints* (VERs). These are voluntary limits on the amount that one country exports to another, usually demanded by the importing country and agreed to by exporters who fear even harsher restrictions. An example was when Japan agreed to limit its car exports to the US in the 1980s. But in 1994 WTO members voted to phase out such restraints.

Indirect non-tariff barriers. A country may also thwart importers by *bureaucratic obstruction*, such as onerous customs paperwork and deliberate delays (US Trade Representative 2019).

Next, a country may impose onerous *standards* on imported goods, sometimes requiring multiple certifications from different government agencies (Fisher 2021). The justification might be to block imports made under poor human or animal welfare conditions, or to ensure the safety and quality of imported goods. And there may be legitimate concerns regarding intellectual property, for example: perhaps foreign competitors are undercutting domestic producers by not paying royalties on patents they use in manufacturing, or are importing and then copying technology. Standards are the most common form of trade barrier, and arguably much more important today than tariffs or quotas. But standards requirements on imports are easily manipulated for purely protectionist reasons.

Even less transparently, governments may subsidise their industries or give them cheap loans, low rents or special tax concessions, making their products cheaper and more attractive than imported ones. Or they may choose only domestic suppliers when they buy things for civil-service or public use (e.g. software, maintenance services, fire-fighting equipment, construction materials and medicines). In some cases (e.g. defence and communications equipment) there may be honest security concerns about buying from abroad; but these concerns are easily stretched to non-strategic industries, despite WTO rules against it.

Which firms to protect?

Countries cannot protect themselves against all imports – that would just create widespread shortages and price rises. Instead, they usually aim to protect what they regard as industries under particular threat from competition, or industries they see as key – such as existing 'national champions' or new 'infant' industries they hope to grow for the future.

But deciding which industries are under threat is not easy. Businesses may struggle, and jobs may be threatened, for many reasons other than foreign competition. They may simply lag behind on investment and productivity. Onerous taxes and regulations might make their product too expensive. Perhaps the market is saturated, or mine lodes are running out, or technology has moved on and people no longer value their product. Whatever the real reasons, foreign competition is usually the scapegoat. The sad result is that protectionism tends to be focused on declining industries rather than growing ones, making it a costly, thankless and ineffective policy.

Nor are governments good at identifying leading-edge firms and technologies. For example, Japan's Ministry of International Trade and Industry (MITI) – widely cited as a successful example of such industrial strategy – probably did more to protect losers than help winners; while South Korea started to boom only *after* it dismantled its protectionist controls (Krueger 2020). And supporting 'national champions' can simply make them lazy and less able to compete.

> Governments are bad at picking winners, but losers are good at picking governments.
>
> — Matt Ridley (2020)

Unintended consequences

Unfortunately, while trade barriers may shelter jobs in some industries, they impose costs on others, such as those that rely on imported raw materials and components for their production processes.

Furthermore, the costs of trade barriers are paid by domestic consumers, in the higher prices they face for imported goods and in reduced choice and competition. For example, 98 per cent of footwear sold in the US is imported. If tariffs eliminated footwear imports, there would be no chance of domestic producers filling the gap before Americans were literally on their uppers.

Protectionism brings other problems, as illustrated by America's 2018 'Trump Tariff' of 25 per cent on steel imports, designed to reverse the loss of Midwest steel jobs. In fact, those job losses reflected a cyclical glut in world steel production, which greater US output would simply worsen. Enforcing the restrictions required a large bureaucracy and led to costly appeals and court cases. Specialist steels that could not be produced in the US were caught up in the tariffs, requiring complicated exemptions to be devised. As the prices of US-made steel rose above world prices, the prices of cars and domestic goods made with steel rose too, making foreign imports more attractive. Overall, the manufacturing job losses probably exceeded any gained in steelmaking, and both wages and GDP suffered (York 2020).

Protectionism imposes costs on other nations too. For instance, high barriers on agricultural imports, such as those imposed by the EU, can be particularly damaging for developing countries that depend on exporting a single crop such as sugar or coffee. When the EU banned the import of shrimp from Benin, it led to the collapse of Benin's shrimp industry, including exporters, fish merchants and fishermen themselves, many of whom were too heavily invested in the industry to find realistic alternatives. The damage persisted long after the ban was eventually lifted (Houssa and Verpooten 2013).

Economists largely agree that the best policy would be a multilateral easing of all protections, as was attempted in the 1986–93 Uruguay Round of GATT, though with little success: countries' political and cultural loyalty to agriculture (even where it is a relatively small industry) is very strong.

The cost of protectionism

With millions of different products being traded, protectionist governments face a complex task in deciding which barriers to apply to each, and an impossible task in doing so fairly. That leads to disputes and court cases and can encourage the corruption of public officials as traders try to keep their particular products out of the controls.

Trade barriers also make smuggling profitable. Goods may be landed clandestinely, or shipped to a third country that is outside the controls and imported from there. They may be mislabelled as goods that are not subject to high quotas or tariffs, or under-invoiced to avoid *ad valorem* tariffs. Again, customs officers may be bribed to overlook these practices and let the goods in.

Setting and policing trade barriers, and countering smuggling and corruption, requires a large bureaucracy. The US, for example, employs 65,000 Customs and Border Protection officers. The EU has 114,000 customs officers working at airports, border crossings, ports and offices. Worldwide, there may be something between half a million and a million customs officers. Not all will be engaged on policing customs barriers – some might be trying to stop the entry of drugs and terrorists – but most probably are. That is a large cost to the world economy.

9 ARGUMENTS FOR PROTECTIONISM

The infant industries argument

As mentioned, one of the most common justifications for trade barriers is to enable countries to grow new industries to a size where they can benefit from large-scale production and compete against established competitors abroad. Developing countries once saw this as crucial to their 'import substitution' policies, outlined in chapter 7; and it might still be important to countries that need to diversify, such as those dependent on a single crop or mineral, the price of which may fluctuate.

History suggests that protectionism can indeed benefit infant industries in emerging economies. Even the US seems to have benefited, in its early years, by using import controls to build up its manufacturing strength. Today too, there might be a case for a country protecting its small-scale producers from transnational corporations, which may be hard for individual countries to regulate (see chapter 12) and so might acquire great market power which they can use to squeeze out potential competitors.

But there are problems with the infant industry argument. For example, which new 'infant' industries should be grown? The choice may be made for political purposes more than any real prospect of economic success. Also, because they are protected, the sheltered industries may become inefficient and slow to mature. Nor is it obvious when they will have matured enough for controls to be removed; and these industries will probably campaign to keep their protections. 'The so-called infants never grow up,' wrote the economist Milton Friedman (1997). 'Once imposed, tariffs are seldom eliminated.' And of course, there remains the cost to consumers who are being denied cheaper imports.

> Tariffs are taxes that a country places on its own citizens for purchasing designated foreign goods; in essence, they hike up the prices of imported products in order to encourage people to buy domestic products instead.
>
> — Fred Hochberg (2020)

If the aim is to grow new industries, there may be better tools: tax concessions, training grants or subsidies may be more effective and less likely to bring on retaliation. In terms of dealing with the market power of global companies, economists generally concur that international agreements on competition policy are a better solution than allowing individual countries to erect a multiplicity of trade barriers.

Anti-dumping argument

Another argument for protectionism is that foreign countries might 'dump' goods on others – exporting them at a price that is lower in the importing country than in their own – in a predatory move designed to damage foreign producers or even drive them out of business and then capture the trade for themselves.

A transnational corporation may have considerable market power that it can use in an effort to squeeze out smaller competitors. But to stifle *all* the world's other producers, such a corporation would need very deep pockets; and if there is little chance of succeeding, it is hard to see why they would try. Predatory dumping by transnational corporations may be rarer than imagined.

The real problem, however, is when governments subsidise their industries or manipulate their currency in order to undercut other nations. They may even use exploited or slave labour to produce export goods at very low cost. China, for example, has been accused of all three by the US, EU and other countries. In this case, international law allows a country to raise a countervailing duty (CVD) on products that are subsidised by exporting nations, so robbing the subsidised exports of any advantage.

However, government subsidies are not always easy to identify, and importing nations may well overestimate them in order, for protectionist reasons, to impose CVDs that are higher than justified. There are also many reasons, other than subsidies, why the price of imported products might be low, even below production cost. Exporters might have produced goods but failed to sell them, or might have a temporary overstock to clear, so unload them cheaply for whatever they can raise. Such one-off or temporary inflows of cheap goods may not harm domestic producers, though they bring short-term benefit to consumers (Anderton 2015). 'Anti-dumping' measures may therefore do more harm than good, fuelling protectionism, which in turn prompts further retaliation (Ikeson 2017).

Labour standards

People in richer countries also complain that the only reason why poorer ones are cheaper is because they have lower employment standards – such as low pay, long hours, unsafe working conditions and child labour. They may have lower taxes on earnings, companies and capital too.

But because capital is scarce in poorer countries, workers' productivity is low, making them more willing, out of necessity, to work longer for less pay and in more dirty and dangerous conditions than those in rich ones. Raising import controls against what they produce merely prevents them from earning, acquiring capital and improving their lives.

Product standards and biosecurity

Another common concern is to keep out products that are potentially unsafe (e.g. electrical goods, medicines, recycling waste or GM crops) or unethically sourced (e.g. meat products or prisoner-made manufactures). And countries often impose other standards on how products are produced and processed, such as environmental standards.

It is clearly protectionism if a country imposes stricter standards on importers than on its own producers. But exactly which safety and ethical objections are legitimate and not merely disguised protectionism? For example, are the concerns about America's use of hormones in cattle, its chlorination of chicken, or its exports of genetically modified cereals legitimate health fears or just an excuse to block US agricultural products? And is America justified in refusing meat products from countries with much lower animal welfare standards, or manufactures from those with poor human rights records?

Because imported product standards are so easily used to protect domestic producers rather than for their stated purpose, they are one of the biggest sources of WTO trade disputes. Where there are indeed legitimate concerns about health or safety, other policies (such as seeking international agreement on product safety standards) may be better ways to enforce them (Anderton 2015).

Security concerns

As already mentioned, countries may argue that some industries (such as defence, IT or communications) are too important strategically to be opened up to foreigners. They may ban the export of these technologies and protect their own 'strategic' industries from competition.

Undoubtedly, these are real and legitimate security concerns. They still require close scrutiny if they are not to be used for protectionist reasons and cause economic harm. America's 1920 Jones Act, for example, requires that goods shipped between US ports must be transported on ships that are American built, owned and operated. The stated aim was to ensure that the US maintained a merchant navy that could be repurposed in time of war. In fact, it raised the price of freight transportation by keeping out competition and requiring goods arriving on foreign vessels to be reloaded onto American ships. This hit distant parts, such as Hawaii and Puerto Rico, particularly badly. Meanwhile, ships became more costly to build because of the rules on American involvement, prompting shipping companies to run them for longer, until they were well past military use. Far from protecting American shipping, the Jones Act largely destroyed it (Krueger 2020: ch. 13).

Sanctions

Trade barriers can be used as a political weapon – to weaken the economy of potentially or actively hostile powers, or to prompt a change in their behaviour. Trade wars may even be used as a trial of strength between hostile countries – less damaging than outright military conflict, but damaging, nonetheless. That point convinces many people that countries should aim to be self-sufficient in essential goods, such as food, in order to protect themselves against the possibility of their supplies being cut off through conflict – not just conflicts between themselves and other countries, but conflicts between other nations that disrupt international trade in their region. Import controls are needed, runs the argument, to ensure that domestic industries can sustain the nation in such a situation.

One special case is the erection of trade barriers when international political conflicts arise and normal diplomatic negotiations break down. An example is the 2006 UN *trade embargo* against Iran, which sought to pressure Iran into halting its uranium enrichment programme. Under an embargo, all imports from (and sometimes exports to) another country are banned, which can have a powerful effect on trading nations.

Trade sanctions may be the only way (short of war) to bring pressure on rogue governments, such as those with poor human rights records. But it is important to ensure that sanctions are not hiding protectionism behind a noble purpose. To avoid such accusations, countries often seek a UN resolution to impose international trade barriers, providing them with a measure of international legitimacy.

However, sanctions may not hit the right target anyway. Rich government elites may be largely unaffected by them, while ordinary citizens may face higher prices or shortages of imported goods, sometimes essential ones including food and medicines. Though trade wars are better than military wars, it seems best to try to avoid both and keep trade open as a way of encouraging mutual dependence and understanding.

10 BALANCE OF PAYMENTS DEFICITS

The balance of payments

Another reason why a country might be tempted to raise trade barriers against another is a shortfall (or *deficit*) in the *balance of payments* between them.

A country's balance of payments is the account of all its international transactions over a certain period. The part recording the transactions that are exports and imports of goods and services is called the *current account*. The transactions in assets, such as land and property or stocks and bonds, is called the *capital account*. (Some economists separate this element further, using 'capital account' only for the non-financial assets and 'financial account' for financial assets.)

A country that imports a greater value of goods and services than it exports has what is called a *current account deficit* (sometimes loosely called a *balance of payments deficit*). It is paying out more for imports than it receives for exports. But, of course, that shortfall has to be paid for; and if all transactions are correctly recorded, the current account deficit must be balanced by an equal surplus in the capital account. Quite simply, a country that spends more on imports than it receives for its exports must sell assets, or go into debt, to fund the difference. Such a situation can pose political difficulties since it makes it appear that a country is not paying its way.

The deficit could of course be closed by earning more from exports or spending less on imports. Sadly, that idea might tempt the country's politicians into protectionism. They might subsidise their export industries, for example, making their goods cheaper to foreign customers, or impose tariffs and quotas on imports, making foreign goods less attractive or less available to home consumers.

> To give Adam Smith's case against mercantilism in extreme concision: imports are Christmas morning; exports are January's MasterCard bill.
>
> — P. J. O'Rourke (2007)

Deficits are not always a problem

However, a balance of payments deficit is not always a problem. If the country can continue to pay the interest on its debts and uses the money to finance investments that produce rising prosperity, it can continue to run deficits and repay its debts when those investments pay off – just like a business taking out a loan to buy new equipment that will improve its output.

In the nineteenth century, for example, the US ran big deficits but invested in oil exploration and in roads and railways that would enhance transport and trade; by the end of World War I, it had become the world's leading exporter. By contrast, in the 1990s a number of South East

Asian countries borrowed more than their growth could sustain, and then borrowed more to cover the interest on their debts. Their mounting deficits led to the 1997–98 'Asian Crisis'.

Deficits may also reflect natural market changes rather than bad policy. Britain, for example, exports oil and chemicals, which are traded in dollars internationally. Before the 2016 Brexit vote, the dollar prices of these goods fell, which reduced Britain's export earnings and so increased its deficit. But after the vote to leave the EU, the value of the British pound fell against the dollar. So now, the dollars that Britain's exports brought in would buy more at home, while imports (now costlier in sterling) fell, all helping to reduce the deficit.

Savings and investment can also affect a country's deficit. People's savings provide the funds that businesses need in order to invest in their production. If savings fall below what firms are investing, firms need to source more capital from abroad. And if people spend rather than save, that raises demand and sucks in imports. The result is a higher current/financial account deficit.

A shortage of domestic savings to fund companies' investment is one reason why the US runs the world's largest persistent deficit. (Though exceptionally, it can fund that overspending merely by printing dollars, which keep their value because they are in constant demand as the main currency of international trade.) By contrast, Germany runs the world's largest trade *surplus*, partly because the creation of the euro favoured its exporters, but also because of high domestic savings. Japan too has a glut of savings over investment, so savers and fund managers have to look abroad for more profitable investment, giving Japan a current account surplus but a capital account deficit.

Country-to-country deficits

Because a country's balance of payments with the world is the result of so many different factors and may be perfectly benign, the mere existence of a deficit is a bad excuse for protectionism. A country's deficit with any single other country is an even worse excuse – though politicians use it often. US President Donald Trump, for example, cited his country's trade deficits with China and Mexico as reasons to renegotiate trade deals and raise import barriers.

But it should be no surprise that one country runs deficits with another, since it may run surpluses with yet others. The US, for example, imports clothes, electronics and cars from some countries but exports food, oil, financial services and aircraft to others. It runs deficits with China, Mexico and Canada, but surpluses with Australia, Britain, Brazil and Argentina. To take a simple analogy: I run a deficit with my hairdresser, to whom I pay money for haircuts, though the hairdresser buys nothing from me. But then I run a surplus with my employers, who pay for my labour though I buy nothing from them.

Bilateral trade figures are also distorted by a counting peculiarity. The nationality of foreign goods is recorded as the last country they come through – even if that final stage contributes only a part of their final value. Often, the final country is China, where many products are assembled and packaged, which misleadingly exaggerates China's surplus with countries such as the US (Hochberg 2020).

Exchange rates

Another of Donald Trump's criticisms of China was that it kept the value of its currency artificially low, making Chinese exports cheaper for Americans and America's exports more expensive for the Chinese.

The exchange rate is the price of one currency in terms of another: how many pounds or euros or roubles you can get for a dollar, say. Today, most currencies are traded openly in foreign exchange ('forex') markets; and just like any other market good, their values are determined by supply and demand. If people round the world are keen to buy American goods, for example, they will need to buy dollars to pay American producers for them, pushing up the price of the dollar. If Americans want to buy foreign goods, they will have to sell dollars to buy the foreign currencies needed to pay for them, and the price of dollars will fall.

Rates also reflect short-term fluctuations in supply and demand. In a hard winter, for instance, the currency of sunny tourist destinations may rise as more people book holidays. Or if a country's central bank raises interest rates, investors may buy more of its currency in order to invest there and reap the higher interest. Markets also reflect speculation: for example, if speculators believe that a country's currency is likely to fall (e.g. because of political uncertainty like Britain's 2016 Brexit vote), they may sell it in anticipation.

Government intervention

But as well as these market pressures, governments also manipulate foreign exchange markets, buying or selling different currencies, including their own, in order to influence prices. They may do this to try to calm volatility in the market caused by some temporary disruption, or to restore investor confidence in their economy.

But they may also manipulate exchange rates for trade advantage, as Trump accused China of doing. Most commonly, they may seek to give their currency an artificially low exchange rate in order to boost their exports by making them cheaper for foreigners, and to reduce imports by making them more expensive for domestic customers. However, the easier sales may make exporters complacent and inefficient, while the higher import prices will hurt domestic consumers and sometimes producers too. Moreover, if the devaluation is large and sudden, there may be deeper consequences: when Belarus devalued in 1992 following the breakup of the old Soviet Union supply chains, inflation soared to over 100 per cent and interest rates hit 45 per cent.

In sum, governments can manipulate their currencies in order to seek a trade advantage, but there are limits – beyond which reality reasserts itself, often painfully.

PART FIVE

TRADE TODAY

11 FREE TRADE REDUX

Post-war commitment to trade

However politically tempting protectionism might be in peacetime and however necessary state controls had been during the two world wars, by the end of World War II the Western powers had come to realise that trade barriers were not only self-defeating but had in fact fuelled destructive conflict. Though the Soviet bloc, along with China and South East Asia chose to remain apart, the Western nations collaborated on the 1948 General Agreement on Tariffs and Trade (GATT), aimed at rebuilding their trading networks and making them freer and more open.

GATT was driven by a belief in the benefits of trade, and that greater cooperation could boost understanding and peace between nations. It would be rules-based, and open to anyone who accepted those rules. Protectionism would be discouraged, and any participating country that offered favourable trading terms to another would have to offer the same terms to all (the 'most favoured nation' provision).

The results have been impressive. The number of countries involved has grown from 23 in 1948 to over 160 today (WTO 2016). World tariff rates that in 1947 averaged over

20 per cent (Brown and Irwin 2015), or by some calculations, 40 per cent (World Bank 1987), had fallen to just 2.6 per cent by 2017 (World Bank 2019).

> GATT may be as important for what it represents in terms of process as for what it has accomplished as an institution. The GATT set a standard for commercial policies and stood as a reminder that striving for the objective of freer multilateral trade was worthwhile. As a set of rules, the GATT provided some credible assurance that tariff levels could move in only one direction ...
>
> — Douglas A. Irwin (1995)

Trade liberalisation was helped by a series of political reforms that brought major nations into the world trading network, and reduced barriers to the flow of investment, people and ideas. Thus, China liberalised soon after the death of Mao Zedong in 1976; in Europe the Berlin Wall fell in 1989 and Eastern bloc nations started trading independently with the West; developing countries started to abandon import substitution policies in favour of more open trade; India introduced liberalising economic reforms in 1991; and the European Union moved to a tariff-free 'single market' in 1993.

Broadening horizons

From 1948 on, GATT's membership grew substantially, as did its reach. In the late 1980s, it had started to make breakthroughs in agriculture (always one of the most contentious issues) and in services, which had become a much more important component of world trade, fuelling concerns about professional standards, intellectual property and copyright.

GATT was primarily a series of negotiating rounds, but in the 1980s, many people felt that it could work better by becoming a formal international body. This led to the creation of the WTO in 1995 and the expansion of negotiations on subsidies, intellectual property, product standards and other issues. Expert WTO panels now rule on trade disputes, and while countries cannot be forced into compliance, they can face retaliation if they do not.

Another factor behind the creation of the WTO was industrialised countries' concerns that their commitment to high employment, welfare and ethical standards meant that they were being undercut by developing countries that maintained less rigorous standards. They hoped that the new body would help nations deal with this.

In addition, production had become truly international, with the emergence of global value chains that included not just the increasingly global production of physical components, but inputs such as design, investment finance, assembly, transportation, marketing and distribution. There was a desire to reflect these inputs in trade negotiations and to ensure quality standards across the entire process. This was important, because while some standards are set by the industries themselves, others are laid down by governments; and with production chains spread across many countries, problems in one country can disrupt whole networks.

Different approaches

Protectionism is still common, but international trade has in general become more free. Different countries and regions have found different ways of liberalising their trade, albeit at a pace that recognises the domestic political realities.

Asian interventionism. Even the Asian tiger economies were hardly models of pure free-market liberalism. Their governments often identified the sectors where the country was likely to have a comparative advantage in exports, and steered investment into them. As already mentioned, the leading example is Japan's Ministry of International Trade and Industry (MITI), though its overall job-creating success is exaggerated: we cannot know which other industries might have succeeded even better if resources had not been steered elsewhere. Also, Japan may not be a model for other countries because its economy was more integrated and therefore easier to control from the centre.

China too opened up its markets to international trade after the reforms of 1978 and is now a huge exporting country that has grown fast as a result. Again, it has not left its export strategy to chance but intervenes greatly – subsidising leading industries such as solar panels, for example, and (critics argue) manipulating its currency to make its products more attractive to importers. This may benefit the sectors concerned – but comes at a cost to Chinese consumers and taxpayers.

Special economic zones. Another strategy used in Asia and elsewhere to promote growth through trade is the creation of special economic zones (SEZs). These areas aim to promote trade and inward investment by applying more generous rules than might be available elsewhere. There are roughly 3,000 SEZs around the world today. They include freeports such as Macau, Hong Kong and Singapore; and zones such as Shannon in Ireland, which specialise in importing goods or components, processing or assembling them, and then re-exporting them again, without subjecting them to the normal customs bureaucracy.

SEZs can allow countries to avoid complete openness to foreign competition, while still admitting it in managed ways. They also allow foreign investors some protection against onerous local taxes or regulations (Poon and Rigby 2017: ch. 6).

Regional trading arrangements. Another halfway house between complete protectionism and open trade with the world are regional trading arrangements. This is where a group of countries enter into an FTA, allowing an agreed range of goods (or all goods) to be imported and exported between them with few barriers. The US, for example, has FTAs with Costa Rica, El Salvador, Guatemala, Honduras, Nicaragua and the Dominican Republic, while the EU has FTAs with Norway, Iceland, Switzerland and Liechtenstein.

Ideally, a regional trade agreement should reduce protectionism between the partners while doing no harm to non-members. But this is not always the case. The EU, for example, is a *customs union* in which the participating members agree to free trade between each other but impose common tariffs against the rest of the world. The customs-free internal ('single') market therefore promotes competition, specialisation and trade between the EU members, bringing both welfare and efficiency gains, and cutting customs bureaucracy. However, the EU's high tariffs on orange juice, dairy and other agricultural goods are clearly protectionist measures to benefit EU farmers. Yet, however unjust that is to farmers in poorer countries, no EU member may offer them better terms.

Nor does the absence of internal tariffs mean trade between the partners is completely free; on the contrary, EU members often use non-tariff barriers such as bureaucratic delays or onerous product standards paperwork in order to resist imports from their supposed partners (Fisher 2021).

Examples of regional trade agreements

There are over 400 trade agreements around the world, though not all are *free trade* agreements. Where there are common interests, history or language, regional agreements may be relatively easy to create. Yet trade blocs can splinter if large differences emerge between member countries, such as diverging debt levels, inflation or tax policy, or simply outlook – as in the case of Britain leaving the EU.

The following examples show how diverse such agreements are, and how dependent they are on the politics within their member countries. For instance, the proposed deal between the US and the EU, potentially the world's largest, foundered largely due to competition concerns from US manufacturers and standards objections from EU unions and environmental groups.

The examples also reflect the importance of geopolitics – as in the attempts by South East Asian countries to become less dependent on Western customers or of China to reduce America's influence in the Pacific Rim. Free trade for its own sake remains a distant dream in much of the world.

European Union (EU). Dating back to the original coal and steel agreements in the 1950s, the 27 EU nations form what is now the most integrated trading bloc in the world, many sharing the same currency (the euro) and all being part of a single market with broadly common standards and regulations. However, there are gaps in the single market (such as services) and numerous non-tariff barriers cause friction for internal trade. The bloc also maintains high protectionist tariffs against agricultural imports in particular.

North American Free Trade Agreement (NAFTA). In 1994 Canada, the US and Mexico formed the world's largest FTA. Business travel was eased, many tariffs were eliminated, and the three granted each other 'most favoured nation' status (meaning they could not give each other less favourable terms than they gave other countries). They also set up a dispute resolution mechanism. The agreement increased trade and brought lower prices.

United States–Mexico–Canada Agreement (USMCA). In 2017, NAFTA was renegotiated, largely under pressure from the US, which was concerned about manufacturing jobs moving to Mexico. Some quotas and tariffs on manufactures were raised, though there were also new agreements on environmental and employment standards, and on digital trade and intellectual property.

Association of South East Asian Nations (ASEAN). Created in 1967, this association aimed at promoting trade, growth and development in the region. Out of it in 1989 grew Asia–Pacific Economic Cooperation, an alliance of 21 countries aimed at creating regional markets for agricultural and primary goods. Many of the same participants are members of the 2020 RCEP agreement (below).

Regional Comprehensive Economic Partnership (RCEP). Formed in 2020, this trade agreement brings China, Indonesia, Malaysia and other South East Asian countries into a low-tariff arrangement with US Pacific Rim allies such as South Korea, Australia, New Zealand and the Philippines. It was aimed at deepening value chains in the Pacific at the expense of US influence.

Mercado Común del Sur (MERCOSUR). This is a customs union, created in 1991 between Brazil, Argentina, Venezuela, Uruguay and Paraguay, with other South American countries as associate members. One of the world's fastest growing trade blocs, it allows free movement of people and investment between these countries.

Commonwealth of Independent States (CIS). Initiated in 1991, this group of 12 former Soviet Union countries encourages economic cooperation but also political and military cooperation. Five members operate a customs union, but political events within various members have prevented the creation of a single market.

12 TRANSNATIONAL CORPORATIONS

The huge expansion in world trade has seen the rise of multinational or transnational corporations (TNCs). Being international, they are able to manage the global value chains that have been made possible by worldwide trade partnerships. But some critics argue that TNCs have become too powerful and impossible for national governments to regulate, control and tax.

Managing global value chains

In the production of all sorts of goods today, it has become quite normal to outsource different manufacturing tasks to other countries. TNCs are well placed to bring together the diverse components and services that these global production networks require – including research and development, resource location, manufacture, assembly, sales, marketing, advertising, finance, transport, logistics, waste management, legal advice and much more. They work with and bring together an equally broad array of different organisations, including subsidiaries, contractors, joint-venture partners, agents, advisers, universities, non-profits or government agencies. And they do it across diverse countries with different laws, regulations, taxes, culture and skill levels.

Too often, people imagine that global value chains arise naturally, by themselves. In fact, such highly sophisticated structures do not come together by chance. Someone has to decide which of the many parts of the production process are best sourced from where and from whom. Are there economies of scale if manufacturing is done by a single firm, for example, or is it better divided between specialist firms and countries – technical components being made in skilled-labour countries, say, and assembly done in cheap-labour countries? Whatever the answers, all the various elements in the production chain must be designed, financed, made, assembled, finished, packaged, transported, marketed and sold into a diverse array of countries with diverse rules and diverse consumers. That all takes conscious planning and management by practitioners who have an international reach and a deep, direct and up-to-date understanding of the markets in which they operate. TNCs have all these qualifications.

The origins of TNCs

This is why these sorts of international production chains gave rise to TNCs. It is nothing new. For centuries, raw materials have been produced in one country, exported for processing in a second, then sold on to others. The Medici Bank operated across Europe as long ago as the fifteenth century, providing capital for merchants who operated everywhere in the known world. In the seventeenth century the Dutch East India Company was not just a trading network, but an early TNC, involved in the production of spice, coffee, sugar and wine, and even in shipbuilding (Poon and Rigby 2017: ch. 3). In the eighteenth and nineteenth centuries, cotton fibre was produced in North America and the Caribbean, taken to Britain for spinning and weaving into textiles, then made into clothes that were sold in Europe, South Asia and South America. Some of these operations were made possible only by mercantilist trade controls, the use of military force or slave labour; but the idea of production on a global scale was being planted.

Certainly, the scale of international production has changed. It was boosted by steamships, which made the transportation of goods and components cheaper, quicker and more reliable. Undersea cables for telegraphs, then telephones, telex, fax and finally the Internet made it much easier to manage international operations in real time and cut the costs of coordinating multiple global activities. Soon, TNCs were operating everywhere – starting in oil and mining (e.g. Standard Oil, Shell, Rio Tinto), then manufacturing (Singer, Siemens, Kodak), food (Nestlé, Unilever) and, more recently, services (Microsoft, Visa).

Naturally, for a TNC to exist and succeed, the benefits of international operation have to be greater than the costs and risks of doing so. In earlier times, those risks were high, but access to foreign markets has become easier, cheaper and more secure (thanks partly to international agreements) so the risks and costs have fallen.

Postwar moves to reduce trade restrictions, which prompted countries to focus on their comparative advantage, advanced this internationalisation as producers looked for the best suppliers. From the mid 1980s, cross-border investment, production and partnerships grew rapidly, particularly in developing countries, where over half of foreign direct investment now goes. There is even a so-called 'transnationality index', based on the proportion of foreign assets, sales and employment in the company (UN Conference on Trade and Development 2020). For Finland's Nokia, Britain's Vodafone and America's Anheuser-Busch, for example, it is around 90 per cent.

Uncertain boundaries

On the positive side, international operation allows producers to hedge against market volatility, and to switch global resources from fading markets to growing ones, boosting productivity and progress. But some TNCs have been criticised for using their global structure to move revenues and profits into low-tax jurisdictions – and even to avoid liability for accidents, as Union Carbide did over the 1984 gas explosion at its pesticide plant in Bhopal, India.

Precisely because of their international spread and fragmented operations, the nationality and boundaries of TNCs can be hard to identify. Are Nokia, Vodafone or Anheuser-Busch really Finnish, British and American companies, given that nearly all their operations take place in other countries? Even core functions may not all be concentrated in the formal 'head office' but may be dispersed across the globe. And perhaps no single part of the network knows precisely how every other part functions.

And what of their impact on the places where they operate? Like many other trading centres, Singapore, for example, is highly reliant on TNCs. Does that assure it of a bright economic future, or make it vulnerable to any changes in how a few huge enterprises choose to operate their international business?

There are certainly potential dangers to a country's economy and security when TNCs that operate there are supported by foreign governments and may be acting as agents of the foreign policy of those governments. For example, powerful governments may use their TNCs to build up other countries' economic dependence on them, or to buy goodwill and secure other countries' compliance with their geopolitical or imperialist ambitions. This is a modern manifestation, perhaps, of how the British and Dutch governments used their state-sponsored TNCs in India and Indonesia centuries ago.

Nevertheless, there is strong evidence that, in general, the presence of TNCs is actually good for domestic industries in their partner countries around the world. That is because foreign investment and the sharing of information, ideas, processes and techniques from other countries in the value chain raise domestic productivity, generating growth.

In the UK, for example, a 10 per cent increase in the presence of foreign companies was found to raise the productivity of domestic plants by 0.5 per cent (Haskel et al. 2002). The UK's failing car industry was largely saved in the 1970s–90s by the more efficient Japanese firms Honda, Nissan and Toyota creating new plants there. Again, this might make UK car-making cities potentially vulnerable to political and financial decisions made on the other side of the world; but then the new techniques, enhanced productivity and boost to employment have already been extremely positive for the UK economy.

How powerful are TNCs?

Critics, however, believe that the global scale of TNCs means they cannot be controlled by individual governments and that they can exert huge power over many countries. Around two-thirds of American trade is thought to be led by TNCs, and many other advanced economies have similar reliance on them. They are particularly dominant in manufacturing, such as car making and IT, where scale is needed and production tasks are easily outsourced. They also have a rising influence in services, such as banking, legal and accounting services, where firms around the globe have combined in order to give their international customers the appropriate international advice and support.

> The nation state as a fundamental unit of man's organized life has ceased to be the principal creative force: International banks and multinational corporations are acting and planning in terms that are far in advance of the political concepts of the nation state.
>
> — Zbigniew Brzezinski (1982)

But this influence may be exaggerated precisely because the complexity of global value chains makes it as hard to distinguish between 'foreign' and 'domestic' products as it is to distinguish between 'foreign' and 'domestic' firms. This can lead to double counting.

For illustration, suppose a country produces materials worth $1; it exports them to another country, where they are worked on to create components worth $2; these are then exported to a third country which makes them into finished goods worth $3, before exporting the product to the end customer. Only $3 of value has been created, but the apparent total in the trade record is twice that ($1+$2+$3 = $6). To take a real-world example, most 'US' cars comprise mostly foreign-made components. Hence most of the value is double counted, making it look as if TNCs' contribution to (and influence over) the world economy is much larger than it really is (Hochberg 2020).

13 TRADE AND MORALITY

Two views of trade

To many people, international trade and globalisation are evil. Like other manifestations of capitalism, they are seen as driven by greed and self-interest, not altruism and co-operation. In particular, globalisation is held to benefit only rich countries and big corporations, which are accused of smothering local markets, putting local producers out of business, forcing people in poor countries into sweatshops, forming crony relationships with politicians and using their transnational structure to avoid their responsibilities.

Liberals take a different view. They accept that the economic reality is far from perfect: businesses do indeed acquire privileges through their political cronies, and change does bring disruption. But liberals still believe that this reality is better than the opposite vision, because trade and commerce are founded on voluntary exchange, reciprocity, respect and peaceful cooperation between diverse individuals. Nobody is forced into accepting some collective dream (Butler 2015).

> A trader ... does not treat men as masters or slaves, but as independent equals. He deals with men by means of

a free, voluntary, unforced, uncoerced exchange – an exchange which benefits both parties by their own independent judgment. A trader does not expect to be paid for his defaults, only for his achievements.

— Ayn Rand (1964)

Liberals hold that trade and commerce encourage cooperation because both sides benefit – and because the process rewards people who improve the lives of others by supplying them what they want and need. Also, far from promoting fear and resentment, trade promotes toleration: we benefit from trading even with people we dislike, and through trade we come to understand them better (Butler 2013).

Trade and liberal values

Experiments indicate that the more widespread markets are, the more people trust each other (Heinrich 2016), giving us grounds for optimism that trade promotes cooperation, understanding and trust between nations too. Studies suggest that trade even promotes fairness and equality, discourages nationalism, defuses ethnic and international conflict and promotes peace (Wright 2018). Trading nations are more likely to share liberal values such as personal and political freedom, the primacy of the individual, minimal coercion, the rule of law, openness and free speech (Butler 2015).

Although trade is certainly associated with these liberal values, and with the institutions that express and preserve them (such as civil society, limited government, representative democracy and independent courts), and probably helps to entrench them, it is not necessarily what causes them in the first place. It seems more probable that the adoption of liberal values and institutions are what allow trade (and the prosperity it brings) to flourish and expand.

Thus, the economic historian Deirdre McCloskey points out that, for most of human history, the average human lived at mere subsistence levels. Then, suddenly, from about 1750, average incomes started to take off. By 1800 the average adult world citizen earned about $3 a day. Today it is $50 a day. In that same time, world population has increased sevenfold – meaning that humanity now produces more than a hundred times the wealth it did in 1800. This 'Great Enrichment', says McCloskey, is not explained merely by technical progress. It stems from the growing, liberal ('bourgeois') values of an expanding middle class, eclipsing the aristocratic idea of commerce as demeaning. It is those liberal values that make trade and commerce possible (McCloskey 2007).

And with trade and commerce comes prosperity. Countries with the most economic freedom generally have greater incomes, more growth and lower rates of poverty (Gwartney et al. 2017). Nor has the huge rise in prosperity since 1800 been confined to a rich few. In much of the world, things that were once luxuries – decent housing, sanitation, lighting and heating, spare clothes, travel, leisure, entertainment, fresh meat – have become accessible to all. Machines now take the hard work out of industrial production and home chores. Health, child survival, longevity and education have all improved markedly (Norberg 2017). International trade has played its part in this, sharpening competition and the incentive to innovate and improve.

Trade and equality

Critics, however, complain that trade might be making inequality worse. Certainly, when trade barriers fall and markets expand, jobs will be shed in less competitive industries. In the richer countries, many of those job losses will be among lower-skilled workers, which may well contribute to rising inequality. Trade may be fine for well-off New York investment bankers, say the critics, but it is disastrous for lower-paid Midwest textile workers. And perhaps the same is happening internationally as some countries prosper and others fall further behind.

But we should not exaggerate the job losses, and any consequent inequality within a rich country, that may be due to trade. Any rise in rich-country inequality (and measurements of inequality are controversial) is the result of many factors: trade explains very little of it (Lawrence 2008). As mentioned earlier, the vast majority of job losses are due to productivity improvements, not trade (Hicks and Devaraj 2015; Devaraj et al. 2017). The minority that are due to trade – and in particular, to trade agreements that see jobs suddenly shifting abroad – are likely to be temporary, and workers will find other, more productive jobs.

Internationally, far from the world's poorest falling further behind, there have been some spectacular successes

– workers in China and South East Asia and South Asia, for instance, now enjoy growing incomes and greater security, while members of India's lowest castes now have well-paying jobs in IT, which values their talent. Indeed, the rise in the incomes of the world's poorest since world trade started to expand in the 1980s has been one of humanity's most astonishing success stories: global income inequality has *decreased* for the first time since the Industrial Revolution (Milanovic 2013).

Studies reveal other benefits of trade for poor countries too. In the 1950s, as already mentioned, Singapore, Hong Kong, South Korea and Taiwan were relatively poor developing nations. Now these 'Asian Tigers' are among the richest places on the globe. Developing economies in general have seen accelerating growth, and are catching up fast, in terms of what they produce and how they produce it, with the advanced ones. Poverty is falling, employment is rising and the quality of life is improving (Dollar and Kraay 2004). While famines caused by wars and natural disasters still occur in the very poorest countries, famines due to crop failures have been virtually eliminated nearly everywhere, thanks to trade allowing food to be supplied across international borders and improved farming techniques (such as GM crops) to expand.

The moral value of trade

Morality is an idea that can apply only to the actions of free individuals. A person who is forced to act in some way, even in a beneficial way, cannot be said to have moral agency.

Free societies, free markets and free trade are therefore necessary for moral action. They also provide countless opportunities for individuals to exercise their moral judgement: in particular, they encourage *good* moral acts, and millions of them.

Moral behaviour and trustworthiness are essentials in exchange. Nobody will return to a supplier who has given them bad value; and they will warn off their friends. This is true particularly for service industries, which involve direct contact between individuals, and which form an increasing proportion of world trade.

Trade encourages people to improve their ability to work with and get along with others, even traditional enemies. Globalisation has seen an increase in tolerance, precisely because of the benefits that trade brings to individuals, groups and countries who may not otherwise agree on much. Trade systematically drives out discrimination based on nationality, ethnicity, colour, gender, sexual orientation, caste and everything else – since those who refuse to deal with others on such grounds do not get the full benefits of truly global trade. For example, the rapid expansion of world trade since the 1980s has spread toleration for different lifestyles. It has also contributed to a rise in the status of women, particularly young women, to a far greater extent than other possible factors such as democracy (Stroup 2008). And with that, trade has improved female life expectancy, literacy and gender equality. On these measures, there can be little doubt that trade is a force for good.

PART SIX

THE FUTURE OF TRADE

14 TRENDS AND LESSONS

The benefits of international trade

Prosperity. Economic life today has been globalised – or more correctly, given the relatively free trade of the nineteenth century, reglobalised. The movement of people, goods, services, components, capital, techniques, technologies, ideas, cultures and values is more rapid and more widespread than it has ever been. Global value chains touch all of us, changing how we work and the products we use in our daily lives. New 'emerging markets' have sprung up in formerly poor countries that now have more access to foreign capital investment, employment options and indeed consumer opportunities: through their integration into global trade networks, they have grown rapidly, with the world's poorest people gaining most – $2-a-day poverty does not seem long for this world.

Choice. Yet growth and incomes tell only half the story. Trade has also given people better quality and better value products, plus worldwide choice. By some estimates, the average US supermarket now has 47,000 products, many of which could not possibly be sourced at home but can only be grown or made in other countries. Shops in less wealthy countries too are now full of international products that were simply unknown before the start of the globalisation era in the early 1990s.

Quality of life. More than that, trade has improved humanity's quality of life, bringing people better access to medicines and healthcare, education, travel, work opportunities, cultural and leisure products such as music, theatre and sport, and much else. The contacts made through trade have enabled ideas, inventions, capital and better productive techniques to spread across the globe, bringing with them progress and improved living standards.

Accelerating progress. The connections that diverse populations make through trade allow them to observe and learn from the ideas, insights and methods of others. That brings forward life-enhancing inventions: a Covid-19 vaccine, for example, was created in days by a German company founded by the children of Turkish immigrants, teamed up with a US transnational corporation that drew in scientific knowledge and processing capacity from around the world (Hendershott et al. 2021). And more broadly, the sharing of knowledge and combining of different insights and concepts accelerates the pace of innovation, and the impact that has on human progress in a never-ending virtuous spiral.

Trust and peace. Equally important, this greater contact through trade has generally created greater trust and toleration between distant peoples, promoted the peaceful resolution of disputes, fostered democracy and open government, and strengthened the principles and institutions upon which these benefits rest.

Resilience of trade. Certainly, issues persist. Emerging economies may still be fragile; there remain doubts about the exploitation of workers, about environmental damage, the survival of cultures, and even whether pandemics are likely to be a bigger problem in an interdependent world. There are setbacks, like financial crises and trade wars. There are security concerns that prompt countries to aim for greater self-sufficiency instead of relying on essentials coming from abroad, arguments about the production and ethical standards of imported products, and doubts about the professional standards of foreign service providers such as bankers, accountants, physicians and others. And there remains considerable protectionism, often achieved in ways that are difficult to see and hard to quantify.

These are all significant concerns that must be taken seriously. But the long-term trend seems clear, that because of its many benefits, trade will continue to expand, contributing to world growth and prosperity.

Trends and challenges

Among the hundreds of nations that now participate in international trade talks, there is a widespread commitment to reducing trade restrictions. Nevertheless, each of them still has plenty of concerns that block the spread of completely open world trade; and the nature of trade changes over the years (e.g. services are now much more important in trade than they once were), throwing up new challenges, among them the following.

Security. There is an increasing focus on issues such as security and the transfer of advanced technology to other (possibly rival or hostile) countries. As high-tech goods are manufactured and traded across the globe, it becomes easier for some countries to access and exploit technologies devised by others. For example, countries that buy IT from China are increasingly concerned about the security implications – such as whether this makes it easy for China to install spyware in their communications networks.

Environment. Concern about climate and the use of fossil fuels is also having an effect on the pattern of trade as countries explore alternative energy sources. For example, the solar energy market has been dominated by China, Japan, Korea and Germany, but now other governments are pouring subsidies into their own countries' green energy research and development. That might be good business, given the rising demand for renewables; but it is quite contrary to the principles of free trade.

In any case, a better policy may be to make use of price incentives and comparative advantage, such as forging world agreement on carbon taxes, which will prompt the development of tradeable alternative energy in those countries best suited for it.

Services. A growing proportion of trade today is not trade in goods, but in services such as consultancy, finance, accounting, law, communications, IT, architecture and construction, publishing, distribution, design, education, health and social care, tourism and conservation, environmental management and transport. International finance too is now an important component of international trade, with financial firms combining worldwide in a bid to serve global value chains.

This development brings new trade policy issues. For example, countries may be unwilling to recognise the credentials of foreign lawyers, accountants or other professionals. That may be due to a genuine concern to maintain high standards; but it is another potential way to favour domestic industries. Every such barrier makes international trade more difficult.

Level playing fields. Standards, more generally, are the main hidden form of protectionism, now that tariffs are discouraged. Though many countries with high employment or environmental standards complain of 'unfair' competition from those with lower standards, and demand a 'level playing field', many of them still subsidise their own export industries through currency manipulation, subsidies, tax concessions or government procurement.

There is really no such thing as a 'level playing field' – countries are simply different. The office workers of a rich country might like a pollution-free environment, while coal miners in a poor one may be more worried about being able to feed their families. Perhaps the best policy is to accept these differences in values and let countries freely exploit their comparative advantage. The benefit of that will be greatest on the very poorest of any country and of the world in general.

Knowledge economy. Today's expanding knowledge economy again features more prominently than before and brings new issues to resolve. Intellectual property protection, for example, is a contentious issue, with richer countries complaining about others counterfeiting their products (something made easier by global outsourcing). And transnational corporations are a major channel by which technology is transferred between countries.

To a liberal, international operations create employment, raise local productivity, improve global equality and prosperity, and advance human progress. Others, however, may see only the downsides of property rights infringements and security threats. Consequently, a number of international dialogues on property rights and security protections have been established, and anti-counterfeiting and intellectual property protections (such as blacklists) now feature prominently in new trade agreements.

South–South trade. Another trend is so-called South–South trade. Historically, trade was dominated by Western Europe and North America, trading with Eastern Europe, Asia, Africa and South America – known as North–South trade. Today, trade is expanding between Asia and South America, for example, and within Asian regions themselves.

Over time, this growth may see Western countries becoming less significant forces within international trade – even though total trade volumes everywhere will probably keep on rising. But concerns remain: is China's development of the Belt and Road project and its heavy investment in Asian and African countries, for example, a genuine advancement of open trade, or a sign of its imperialist ambitions?

Political challenges to free trade policies

Though international trade discussions today may acknowledge the widespread benefits of world trade, they are in reality driven far more by national and international politics.

Domestic politics. A country's economic, social and welfare policies, and the pressure it faces from workers whose jobs are threatened by foreign competition, are crucial to its stance on trade. Trade can be a convenient scapegoat for an industry's failure to adapt to technological advances, financial upheavals, or changing markets. Culture, ethics and popular opinion can be as important as economics in shaping trade policy, often more so.

However, focusing on the broader benefits of trade is crucial, because it affects the lives not just of businesses but millions of consumers, at home and worldwide.

Geopolitics. Larger geopolitical concerns also distort trade policy. Countries and sometimes groups of countries may use trade as a weapon against hostile countries, or those with poor human rights records, perhaps by denying them essential imports or refusing access to their exports in the hope of making them poorer or building up public pressure to change their policies. Sometimes, regional trade deals are designed largely to reduce the influence of a rich neighbour over local markets. The Trump-era trade disputes between China and America (and others) may even be a symptom of a fundamental clash of visions over how the world's political and economic systems should operate.

Certainly, it is better if countries resort to trade disputes rather than military action. But trade disputes too can cause deep and widespread loss to citizens all over the world.

International framework. An agreed multinational trade framework is vital if the gains from trade are to be generalised. Markets can operate best under a rule of law, where accepted rules of property and contract are followed and enforced. This does not require some sort of world government – merely the agreement of the trading partners.

Despite all the politics that go on in international organisations, the WTO's membership rules and dispute resolution process are probably the best hope for this. The need is urgent, given the expansion of less tangible trade such as trade in services and over the internet, plus rising concerns about human rights, employment standards, intellectual property, security and environmental protection. Sadly, domestic laws struggle to keep up with these developments; the liberalisation of trade in services, for example, has proved one of the most difficult to agree under both GATT and WTO.

The pressure for protection

The study of trade, and trade wars, teaches a clear lesson that protectionism does not create or preserve jobs, and usually has unintended and damaging results. Barriers raise prices for home consumers, reduce the stimulus of competition and starve domestic industries of raw materials.

> Few measures that we could take would do more to promote the cause of freedom at home and abroad than complete free trade ... Sell here what you can and wish to. Buy whatever you can and wish to. In that way cooperation among individuals can be worldwide and free.
> — Milton and Rose Friedman (1997).

Yet the political pressure for protectionism is driven more by perception than fact. Few people in the US, for example, realise that the number of steel jobs at risk from imports is tiny in comparison to the number of jobs in healthcare, restaurants, offices, education, supermarkets, retailing, IT and many more sectors that benefit from trade. And in any case, jobs are lost for many reasons, not just trade – technological changes, new fashions, rising input prices, management mistakes, tax rises or tighter regulations among them.

Unfortunately, the debate on trade policy will always lack balance. Millions of consumers benefit from trade through lower prices and wider choice – a trend so commonplace that we hardly notice it. A much smaller number of people may lose their jobs to foreign competition, but their plight is much more visible in the public debate. Workers will campaign in the streets to protect their jobs, but consumers do not hold rallies to celebrate a few dollars off the price of their groceries or their ability to get fresh fruit in the winter. Policymakers are therefore much more likely to be moved to action by the noisy producer interests than those of the quiet but more numerous consumers (Butler 2012).

The need for adaptability

Economic change is a constant process. Candlemakers were put out of business by gaslights, livery stables by motor vehicles, typesetters by computers, and many shops by online retailers. Artificial intelligence will revolutionise yet more industries. But despite the disruption brought for some, such progress delivers huge improvements to the lives of the general public – which is the whole purpose of production in the first place. Trade simply accelerates this inevitable and beneficial process.

The real policy question, therefore, is how to ensure that change does not come at exorbitant cost to those who are displaced by it. And if governments decide that they must intervene, how to ensure that they focus on helping the affected groups to adjust, rather than prolonging the life of outdated and redundant industries.

Policy needs to keep flexible to accommodate these and other changes. There are huge gains to be grasped: booming changes in agriculture that have almost eliminated famine; industrial progress; falling poverty; rising wealth and equality; science and progress; human understanding and culture; democracy and justice. Free trade and the liberal values on which it is based are crucial in spreading these benefits. They are worth the effort to protect them.

We cannot predict future production and trading patterns, nor the potential for disruptions, when the world is so interdependent. But we can at least prevent laws from locking us into past realities instead of building the flexibility and readiness we need to absorb change, tool up for tomorrow and grasp the opportunities.

Trade has shaped our lives. Even more, it will shape our future.

REFERENCES

Atakuman, C. et al. (2020) Before the Neolithic in the Aegean. *Journal of Island and Coastal Archaeology* (online).

Brooke, J. (1990) Brazil backing computer imports. *The New York Times*, 9 July.

Brzezinski, Z. (1982) *Between Two Ages: America's Role in the Technetronic Era*. Westport, CT: Greenwood Press.

Brown, C. P. and Irwin, D. A (2015) The GATT's starting point: tariff levels circa 1947. National Bureau of Economic Research, Working Paper 21782 (http://www.nber.org/papers/w21782).

Butler, E. (2007) *Adam Smith: A Primer*. London: Institute of Economic Affairs.

Butler, E. (2011) *The Condensed Wealth of Nations*. London: Adam Smith Institute.

Butler, E. (2012) *Public Choice: A Primer*. London: Institute of Economic Affairs.

Butler, E. (2013) *Foundations of a Free Society*. London: Institute of Economic Affairs.

Butler, E. (2015) *Classical Liberalism: A Primer*. London: Institute of Economic Affairs.

Butler, E. (2018) *An Introduction to Capitalism*. London: Institute of Economic Affairs.

Butler, E. (2019) *School of Thought: 101 Great Liberal Thinkers*. London: Institute of Economic Affairs.

Cain, P. J. (1982) Professor McCloskey on British free trade, 1841–1881: some comments. *Explorations in Economic History* 19(2): 201–7.

Cobden, R. (1846) Speech in Manchester, 15 January.

Devaraj, S., Hicks, M. J., Wornell, E. J. and Faulk, D. (2017) How vulnerable are American communities to automation, trade and urbanization? Ball State University Center for Business and Economic Research and the Rural Policy Research Institute Center for State Policy, 19 June.

Dinda, S. (2004) Environmental Kuznets curve hypothesis: a survey. *Ecological Economics* 49(4): 431–55.

Dollar, D. and Kraay, A. (2004) Trade, growth, and poverty. *Economic Journal* 114(493): F22–F49.

The Economist (2020) Oil and commodity prices are where they were 160 years ago, 27 April (https://www.economist.com/graphic-detail/2020/04/27/oil-and-commodity-prices-are-where-they-were-160-years-ago).

Edmonds, E. and Pavcnik, N. (2004) International trade and child labor: cross-country evidence. National Bureau of Economic Research (http://www.nber.org/papers/w10317).

Findlay, R. and O'Rourke, K. (2007) *Power and Plenty: Trade, War and the World Economy in the Second Millennium.* Princeton University Press.

Fisher, M. H. N. (2021) *Reality versus Rhetoric in 'Free' Trade: An Exporter's Tale.* London: Adam Smith Institute.

Frankel, J. A. and Romer, D. H. (1999) Does trade cause growth? *American Economic Review* 89(3): 379–99.

Frankel, J. A. and Romer, D. H. (2005) Is trade good or bad for the environment? Sorting out the causality. *Review of Economics and Statistics* 87(1): 85–91.

Friedman, M. and Friedman, R. D. (1997) The case for free trade. *Hoover Digest*, no. 4.

Gwartney, J., Lawson, R. and Hall, J. (eds) (2017) *Economic Freedom of the World: 2017 Annual Report*. Vancouver, BC: Fraser Institute.

Hartley, C. K. (2008) Trade: discovery, mercantilism and technology. In *The Cambridge Economic History of Modern Britain* (ed. R. Floyd and P. Johnson), vol. 1.

Haskel, J. E, Pereira, S. C. and Slaughter, M. J. (2002) Does inward foreign direct investment boost the productivity of domestic firms? National Bureau of Economic Research (http://www.nber.org/papers/w8724).

Heath, R. and Mobarak, A. (2012) Does demand or supply constrain investments in education? Evidence from garment sector jobs in Bangladesh (https://economics.yale.edu/sites/default/files/files/Workshops-Seminars/Development/mobarak-120416.pdf).

Heinrich, J. (2016) Do markets make us fair, trusting and co-operative, or bring out the worst in us? *Evonomics*, 6 August (https://evonomics.com/do-markets-make-us-fair-trusting-joseph-henrich/).

Hendershott, R., Brook, Y. and Watkins, D. (2021) Ingenuism: a new theory of innovation (https://ingenuism.substack.com).

Hicks, M. J. and Devaraj, S. (2015) *The Myth and the Reality of Manufacturing in America*. Center for Business and Economic Research, Ball State University (http://conexus.cberdata.org/files/MfgReality.pdf).

Hochberg, F. P. (2020) *Trade Is Not a Four Letter Word*. New York: Avid Reader Press.

Houssa, R. and Verpooten, M. (2013) The unintended consequences of an export ban: evidence from Benin's shrimp sector. University of Namur Centre for Research in the Economics of Development, Working Paper 1304.

Ikeson, D. J. (2017) Antidumping 101: everything you need to know about the steel industry's favourite protectionist bludgeon. Cato Institute blog, 27 April (https://www.cato.org/blog/antidumping-101-everything-you-need-know-about-steel-industrys-favorite-protectionist-bludgeon).

Irwin, D. A. (1995) The GATT in historical perspective. *American Economic Review* 85(2): 323–28.

Klein, M. C. (2016) How many US manufacturing jobs were lost to globalisation? *Financial Times*, 6 December (https://www.ft.com/content/66165693-ddf8-3988-b7e2-5ea887303c3e).

Krpec, O. and Hodulak, V. (2019) War and international trade: Impact of trade disruption on international trade patterns and economic development. *Brazilian Journal of Political Economy* 39(1): 152–72.

Krueger, A. O. (2020) *International Trade: What Everyone Needs to Know.* Oxford University Press.

Lawrence, R. Z. (2008) Blue-collar blues: is trade to blame for rising US income inequality? Peterson Institute for International Economics, Washington, DC (https://www.piie.com/bookstore/blue-collar-blues-trade-blame-rising-us-income-inequality).

Mankiw, G. (2006) Outsourcing redux. *Greg Mankiw's Blog*, 7 May (http://gregmankiw.blogspot.com/2006/05/outsourcing-redux.html).

McCaig, B. and Pavcnik, N. (2014) Export markets and labor allocation in a low-income country. National Bureau of Economic Research (http://www.nber.org/papers/w20455).

McCloskey, D. (2007) *The Bourgeois Virtues: Ethics for an Age of Commerce.* University of Chicago Press.

McDowell, A. (1999) *Laundry Lists and Love Songs: Village Life in Ancient Egypt.* Oxford: Clarendon Press.

Milanovic, B. (2013) Global income inequality in numbers: in history and now. *Global Policy* 4(2): 198–208.

Mohan, S. (2010) *Fair Trade without the Froth.* London: Institute of Economic Affairs.

Norberg, J. (2017) *Progress: Ten Reasons to Look Forward to the Future.* London: Oneworld Publications.

OECD (2019) Trade in fake goods is now 3.3% of world trade and rising. Newsroom, 18 March (https://www.oecd.org/news room/trade-in-fake-goods-is-now-33-of-world-trade-and-ris ing.htm).

Ohlin, B. (1933) *Interregional and International Trade.* Harvard University Press.

O'Rourke, K. (1997) The European grain invasion, 1870–1913. *Journal of Economic History* 57(4): 775–801.

O'Rourke, K. (1999) British trade policy in the 19th century: a review article. University College Dublin, Department of Political Economy Working Paper (http://econpapers.repec.org/paper/fthdublec/99_2f22.htm).

O'Rourke, P. J. (2007) *On the Wealth of Nations.* Old Saybrook, CT: Tantor Media.

O'Rourke, P. J. (2009) Mr Right. *New Zealand Herald,* 17 April.

Pirie, M. (2002) *The People Economy*. London: Adam Smith Institute.

Poon, J. and Rigby, J. L. (2017) *International Trade: The Basics*. Abingdon: Routledge.

Rand, A. (1964) The objectivist ethics. *The Virtue of Selfishness*. New York: Signet.

Ricardo, D. (1817) *On the Principles of Political Economy and Taxation*.

Ridley, M. (2010) *The Rational Optimist*. London: Fourth Estate.

Ridley, M. (2020) *How Innovation Works*. London: Fourth Estate.

Schiermeier, Q. (2015) Ancient DNA reveals how wheat came to prehistoric Britain. *Nature* (online: news).

Selkirk, A. (2020) The secret of civilization (http://www.civiliza tion.org.uk).

Sidwell, M. (2008) *Unfair Trade*. London: Adam Smith Institute.

Smith, A. (1759) *The Theory of Moral Sentiments* (https://oll.liber tyfund.org/title/smith-the-theory-of-moral-sentiments-and -on-the-origins-of-languages-stewart-ed).

Smith, A. (1763) *Lectures on Jurisprudence* (https://oll.liberty fund.org/title/smith-lectures-on-justice-police-revenue-and -arms-1763).

Smith, A. (1776) *An Inquiry into the Nature and Causes of the Wealth of Nations* (https://oll.libertyfund.org/title/smith-an -inquiry-into-the-nature-and-causes-of-the-wealth-of-nati ons-cannan-ed-in-2-vols).

Sowell, T. (2002) *The Quest for Cosmic Justice*. New York: Simon & Schuster.

Stiglitz, J. (2007) *Making Globalization Work*. New York: Norton & Company.

Stroup, M. D. (2008) Separating the influence of capitalism and democracy on women's well-being. *Journal of Economic Behavior and Organization* 67: 560–72.

Summerhayes, G. (2009) Obsidian network patterns in Melanesia – sources, characterization and distribution. *Bulletin of the Indo-Pacific Prehistory Association* 29: 109–23.

Terborgh, A. G. (2003) The post-war rise of world trade: does the Bretton Woods System deserve credit? Economic History Working Papers (78/03). Department of Economic History, London School of Economics and Political Science, London (http://eprints.lse.ac.uk/22351/).

US Bureau of Labor Statistics (2020) Labor force statistics from the current population survey, 22 January (https://www.bls .gov/cps/cpsaat32.htm).

UN Conference on Trade and Development (2020) *Transnational Corporations: Investment and Development* 27(2).

US Trade Representative (2019) *National Trade Estimate Report on Foreign Trade Barriers* (https://ustr.gov/sites/default/files/ 2019_National_Trade_Estimate_Report.pdf).

Williams, A. (2019) Bronze Age discovery reveals surprising extent of Britain's trade with Europe 3,600 years ago (https://the conversation.com/bronze-age-discovery-reveals-surprising -extent-of-britains-trade-with-europe-3-600-years-ago-12 5973).

World Bank (2016) Trade (% of GDP) | Data (http://data.world bank.org/indicator/NE.TRD.GNFS.ZS).

World Bank (1987) *World Development Report*, 134-35.

World Bank (2018) World Bank Open Data: Tariff rate, applied, weighted mean, all products (%) (https://data.worldbank.org/ indicator/TM.TAX.MRCH.WM.AR.ZS).

World Bank (2019) World Bank Open Data: Trade (% of GDP) (https://data.worldbank.org/indicator/NE.TRD.GNFS.ZS).

Wright, W. A. (2018) Is commerce good for the soul? An empirical assessment. *Economic Affairs* 38(3): 422–33.

WTO (2016) *World Trade Statistical Review 2016*. Geneva: World Trade Organization (https://www.wto.org/english/res_e/stat is_e/wts2016_e/wts2016_e.pdf).

York, E. (2020) Tracking the economic impact of US tariffs and retaliatory actions. Tariff Tracker, The Tax Foundation (https://taxfoundation.org/tariffs-trump-trade-war/).

FURTHER READING

Anderton, A. (2015) *Economics*, 6th edn. Ormskirk: Anderton Press.

Many economics textbooks have sections on trade. This is one of the best: comprehensive, succinct, direct, fair, with no ideological agenda.

Butler, E. (2011) *The Condensed Wealth of Nations*. London: Adam Smith Institute.

A short, readable summary of Adam Smith's classic 1776 book, including his explanations of the merits of free trade and specialisation and his arguments against mercantilism.

Findlay, R. and O'Rourke, K. (2007) *Power and Plenty: Trade, War and the World Economy in the Second Millennium*. Princeton University Press.

Large, comprehensive study of the history of international trade over the last thousand years. It demonstrates and explains the expansions and contractions in trade, the dependence of trade on geopolitics, the role of wars and other events. And it traces the development of the trading links between Europe and Asia.

Hochberg, F. P. (2020) *Trade Is Not a Four Letter Word*. New York: Avid Reader Press.

Easy-to-read defence of free trade from a former US trade official, this book demonstrates how poor life would be without all the goods we import from other countries. It reviews the misconceptions about trade and, through the life histories of six everyday products, it explains how trade works and how it has changed our lives for the better.

Krueger, A. O. (2020) *International Trade: What Everyone Needs to Know*. Oxford University Press.

Very comprehensive review of all aspects of trade, yet easy to read. It looks at the recent history of trade and the issues facing trade negotiations today, the case for free trade and the ill effects of protectionism, the 'trade deficit' issue, the job-protection issue, currency manipulation, the need for international policy on trade, trade negotiations and remedies, China, developing countries, regional trade deals and much else.

Poon, J. and Rigby, J. L. (2017) *International Trade: The Basics*. Abingdon: Routledge.

Another comprehensive but digestible outline of trade, including its history and theory, transnational corporations, regional trade agreements, the role of trade in development, jobs and other issues, and the likely future directions of trade and trade policy.

Selkirk, A. (2020) The secret of civilization (http://www.civiliza tion.org.uk).

Written from an archaeological point of view, and covering many countries and historical time periods, this provides a full history of trade from the earliest 'gift exchange' trade to markets built on the invention of money.

ABOUT THE IEA

The Institute is a research and educational charity (No. CC 235 351), limited by guarantee. Its mission is to improve understanding of the fundamental institutions of a free society by analysing and expounding the role of markets in solving economic and social problems.

The IEA achieves its mission by:

- a high-quality publishing programme
- conferences, seminars, lectures and other events
- outreach to school and college students
- brokering media introductions and appearances

The IEA, which was established in 1955 by the late Sir Antony Fisher, is an educational charity, not a political organisation. It is independent of any political party or group and does not carry on activities intended to affect support for any political party or candidate in any election or referendum, or at any other time. It is financed by sales of publications, conference fees and voluntary donations.

In addition to its main series of publications, the IEA also publishes (jointly with the University of Buckingham), *Economic Affairs*.

The IEA is aided in its work by a distinguished international Academic Advisory Council and an eminent panel of Honorary Fellows. Together with other academics, they review prospective IEA publications, their comments being passed on anonymously to authors. All IEA papers are therefore subject to the same rigorous independent refereeing process as used by leading academic journals.

IEA publications enjoy widespread classroom use and course adoptions in schools and universities. They are also sold throughout the world and often translated/reprinted.

Since 1974 the IEA has helped to create a worldwide network of 100 similar institutions in over 70 countries. They are all independent but share the IEA's mission.

Views expressed in the IEA's publications are those of the authors, not those of the Institute (which has no corporate view), its Managing Trustees, Academic Advisory Council members or senior staff.

Members of the Institute's Academic Advisory Council, Honorary Fellows, Trustees and Staff are listed on the following page.

The Institute gratefully acknowledges financial support for its publications programme and other work from a generous benefaction by the late Professor Ronald Coase.

Other books recently published by the IEA include:

Taxation, Government Spending and Economic Growth
Edited by Philip Booth
Hobart Paperback 184; ISBN 978-0-255-36734-9; £15.00

Universal Healthcare without the NHS: Towards a Patient-Centred Health System
Kristian Niemietz
Hobart Paperback 185; ISBN 978-0-255-36737-0; £10.00

Sea Change: How Markets and Property Rights Could Transform the Fishing Industry
Edited by Richard Wellings
Readings in Political Economy 7; ISBN 978-0-255-36740-0; £10.00

Working to Rule: The Damaging Economics of UK Employment Regulation
J. R. Shackleton
Hobart Paperback 186; ISBN 978-0-255-36743-1; £15.00

Education, War and Peace: The Surprising Success of Private Schools in War-Torn Countries
James Tooley and David Longfield
ISBN 978-0-255-36746-2; £10.00

Killjoys: A Critique of Paternalism
Christopher Snowdon
ISBN 978-0-255-36749-3; £12.50

Financial Stability without Central Banks
George Selgin, Kevin Dowd and Mathieu Bédard
ISBN 978-0-255-36752-3; £10.00

Against the Grain: Insights from an Economic Contrarian
Paul Ormerod
ISBN 978-0-255-36755-4; £15.00

Ayn Rand: An Introduction
Eamonn Butler
ISBN 978-0-255-36764-6; £12.50

Capitalism: An Introduction
Eamonn Butler
ISBN 978-0-255-36758-5; £12.50

Opting Out: Conscience and Cooperation in a Pluralistic Society
David S. Oderberg
ISBN 978-0-255-36761-5; £12.50

Getting the Measure of Money: A Critical Assessment of UK Monetary Indicators
Anthony J. Evans
ISBN 978-0-255-36767-7; £12.50

Socialism: The Failed Idea That Never Dies
Kristian Niemietz
ISBN 978-0-255-36770-7; £17.50

Top Dogs and Fat Cats: The Debate on High Pay
Edited by J. R. Shackleton
ISBN 978-0-255-36773-8; £15.00

School Choice around the World … And the Lessons We Can Learn
Edited by Pauline Dixon and Steve Humble
ISBN 978-0-255-36779-0; £15.00

School of Thought: 101 Great Liberal Thinkers
Eamonn Butler
ISBN 978-0-255-36776-9; £12.50

Raising the Roof: How to Solve the United Kingdom's Housing Crisis
Edited by Jacob Rees-Mogg and Radomir Tylecote
ISBN 978-0-255-36782-0; £12.50

How Many Light Bulbs Does It Take to Change the World?
Matt Ridley and Stephen Davies
ISBN 978-0-255-36785-1; £10.00

The Henry Fords of Healthcare … Lessons the West Can Learn from the East
Nima Sanandaji
ISBN 978-0-255-36788-2; £10.00

An Introduction to Entrepreneurship
Eamonn Butler
ISBN 978-0-255-36794-3; £12.50

An Introduction to Democracy
Eamonn Butler
ISBN 978-0-255-36797-4; £12.50

Having Your Say: Threats to Free Speech in the 21st Century
Edited by J. R. Shackleton
ISBN 978-0-255-36800-1; £17.50

The Sharing Economy: Its Pitfalls and Promises
Michael C. Munger
ISBN 978-0-255-36791-2; £12.50

Other IEA publications

Comprehensive information on other publications and the wider work of the IEA can be found at www.iea.org.uk. To order any publication please see below.

Personal customers

Orders from personal customers should be directed to the IEA:

IEA
2 Lord North Street
FREEPOST LON10168
London SW1P 3YZ
Tel: 020 7799 8911, Fax: 020 7799 2137
Email: sales@iea.org.uk

Trade customers

All orders from the book trade should be directed to the IEA's distributor:

NBN International (IEA Orders)
Orders Dept.
NBN International
10 Thornbury Road
Plymouth PL6 7PP
Tel: 01752 202301, Fax: 01752 202333
Email: orders@nbninternational.com

IEA subscriptions

The IEA also offers a subscription service to its publications. For a single annual payment (currently £42.00 in the UK), subscribers receive every monograph the IEA publishes. For more information please contact:

Subscriptions
IEA
2 Lord North Street
FREEPOST LON10168
London SW1P 3YZ
Tel: 020 7799 8911, Fax: 020 7799 2137
Email: accounts@iea.org.uk

Notes

Notes

Notes

Notes

Notes

Notes